alba house
DIVISION OF THE SOCIETY OF ST. PAUL
STATEN ISLAND, N.Y. 10314

BERNARD HÄRING REPLIES

answers to 50 moral and religious questions

Bernard Häring, C.Ss.R.

This book was first published by Edizioni Paoline Alba, Italy under the title: *Padre Bernard Häring Risponde*

Nihil Obstat:

John A. Goodwine, J.C.D.
Censor Librorum

Imprimatur:

† Terence J. Cooke, D.D., V.G.

New York, N.Y. - Nov. 22, 1966

Library of Congress Catalog Number: 67-15201.

Designed, printed and bound in the U.S.A. by the Pauline Fathers and Brothers of the Society of St. Paul at Staten Island, New York as a part of their communications apostolate.

Contents

Introduction

This present volume brings together 50 replies — some brief, others more fully developed — recently published in the Society of St. Paul's Italian Catholic magazine, the *Famiglia Cristiana.* Because of its exceptionally wide circulation (over 1 ¾ million copies weekly), the magazine enabled Father Häring to reach an unusually large number of families who took advantage of the opportunity to present to him their problems in a variety of areas. In particular the arguments treated include urgent and practical questions regarding the existence of God, sexual morality within and outside of marriage, confession, the value of celibacy and evangelical poverty in the twentieth century, thorny problems concerning the morality of contraband activities, the suicide of spies, etc. The author, an internationally known moral theologian, is no stranger to life and to the problems of the man on the street. In his replies he does not take a pedantic tone but expresses an uncommon understanding and sensibility for the concrete situations of life in the modern world. The most salient characteristic of these replies lies in the fact that they are never limited to defining solely what is licit and illicit in a human act but go beyond this and illustrate the positive values inherent in the precepts of Christian morality, showing how they reveal their true meaning only when considered in the light of the Gospels and of the commandment of Christ to love God above all things and one's neighbor as oneself.

Preface

Some well-meaning friends of mine told me one day that a student of moral theology who had a world-wide reputation could not afford to squander his precious time by answering popular questions about every-day problems, but ought to devote all his effort to scientific research. For my part, I think of scientific moral theology as a loving and very serious occupation, one which is concerned with all the courses through which the will of God can manifest itself to us, with a view towards making the response that is proper to the divine will. Within the framework of this vocation, the moralist must be especially concerned with the service of life and the realization of salvation in life.

The consideration of letters and questions put to him by his readers proves to be a source of benefit for the moralist himself. They show him the way and manner in which other people feel about moral problems. The questions that people ask him, based on their immediate personal experience, are an integral part of that precious material which, thanks to God's grace, reflects the "signs of the times."

In my answers I have always made a particular effort to insert the individual moral questions within the broader framework of the Gospel teaching. Never have I been content merely with furnishing the reader with some sort of medical prescription designed to be used in a mechanical way. The really important thing is to provide an indication, in every individual case, of the sense and direction of the great commandment of love in such a way that everyone can achieve a personal encounter with it and thus know how to find the right direction for himself and boldly take one step after another along the path of a more and perfect self-realization.

In presenting this collection of replies, I must acknowledge my debt of thanks to those who have supplied me with their various questions, and especially the *Famiglia Cristiana* which has graciously permitted me to thus establish so many bonds of personal friendship with its readers.

Bernard Häring, C.Ss.R.

God

1

HOW CAN IT BE DEMONSTRATED THAT GOD EXISTS? (I)

I would like to know whether the existence of God is demonstrable in terms of irrefutable proofs. If the answer is yes, then please furnish me with such proofs. If, however, it is not possible, I should then like to know a good reason for believing that God exisits and that the Catholic religion is the true one.

An old missionary, who had spent some forty years working among the mountain peoples of Vietnam, was telling me one day how, in the first days of his missionary activity there, he had attempted to prove the existence of God to these simple people by long and closely reasoned arguments. But they proved to be only bored with his long discourses, until one day they told him clearly and simply: "Father, ever since the world began, no one has ever been able to doubt that God exists. What we want to know is simply whether he has been kind enough to have anything to do with poor devils like us."

When someone doubts whether or not God really exists it is very difficult to demonstrate the fact that he does. It is a sad symptom of spiritual poverty and weakness when a man or especially a whole group of persons needs long and difficult proofs to demonstrate the existence of God. It I had a friend who not only spoke to me but even went so far as to give his life in order to save me, it would be an insult and a useless waste of time to keep appealing to proofs that would confirm the fact of his existence. This would be admissible only if he had not ever lived.

Dialogue with God

No one is more alive than God. He is speaking and active in everything, and everything speaks of him. "The heavens proclaim the glory of the Lord." The firmament and the flowers of the field all manifest the infinite power and wisdom of the Creator. The discoveries of modern science and technical research have revealed the existence of marvelous possibilities which could not possibly have been brought into being by mere blind chance. The further we advance in our knowledge of nature, the clearer becomes the voice of its wonderful laws; they go far beyond the level of simple matter and could have been imposed on nature only by an intelligent spirit.

It is almost impossible to make a deaf man understand what music is. In the same way it is almost impossible to explain what man really is to a person who thinks only of eating and drinking, to the utilitarian who looks only for his own advantage, to the pleasure-seeker who thinks only in terms of his own selfish comfort. All these men are necessarily lacking in the thinking and sensitivity proper to fully mature individuals.

In their case, the first thing is to educate them to think and feel in a human way, because only in this way will they be able to understand, or at least to suspect, what it means to be a man. Then they must also be educated to think of others, to pay attention to them, to be grateful and pleasant, to understand how to make them happy. Then they will understand what it means to be a man.

Dialogue with Souls

The man who is sensitive to beauty remains enchanted by it and enjoys it; the man who is sensitive to goodness remains open to the example set by good and altruistic men; the man who harbors pure thoughts and a pure heart and is wholly dedicated to good does not need any proof of the existence of God; in everything he perceives and experiences the ultimate meaning of existence, that is, an ultimate beauty, goodness without end, the personal Thou by whom and to whom he is called.

Here on earth, however, we do not yet contemplate God face to face, and thus our spiritual eye can be obscured by thick clouds. Frequently our will is troubled by poorly regulated desires and our heart is distracted and consumed by an infinity of created things of little value. In these disturbing moments it is some-times absolutely necessary to call to mind the reasons that prove the existence and the nearness of God.

To believe in the existence of God it is not necessary to have a refined cultural sensitivity or a profound philosophical formation, even granted that it is possible to express the proofs for God's existence in the technical vocabulary and specialized terminology of philosophy. But if a philosopher were to try to convince me that I could accept the existence of God, with certainty, only on the basis of his complicated reasoning, I would have serious doubts about his mental faculties, just as I would have serious doubts about the good sense of a doctor in chemistry who would try to demonstrate that I could not breathe unless I was first familiar with the chemical formula for the composition of air; not that I have no use for his formulas, but I can very well breathe fresh air without them.

2

HOW CAN GOD'S EXISTENCE BE DEMONSTRATED? (II)

> *I refer to the question, "How can it be demonstrated that God exists?"*
>
> *I would not cast doubt upon the competence of Father Bernard Häring, but it does seem rather illogical to say: "If I had a friend who not only spoke to me but even went so far as to give his life in order to save me, it would be an insult and a useless waste of time to keep appealing to proofs that would confirm the fact of his existence. This would be admissible only if he had not ever lived."*
>
> *The question is quite different: whether or not it is a fact that he has spoken to me, etc.*
>
> *It also seems rather bold to say that it is a "symptom of spiritual poverty and weakness" to need "long and difficult proofs": the statement is contradicted by the history of many persons who were neither poor nor weak.*

The Church vigorously maintains, and proposes as an article of faith, that "God, one and true, our Creator and Lord, can be known with certainty by means of the natural light of human reason" (Vatican I, Densinger 1806). Now the religious bearing of this text is unjustly limited if we claim that it is possible to arrive at a certain knowledge of the existence of God only with the help of scientific philosophy and its technical vocabulary. The uncorrupted heart and open mind of every normal man, living in everyday normal human society, are sufficient to arrive at a knowledge of the existence of God and to affirm his existence in a perfectly rational manner.

Who can know God

There is a certain cold knowledge, naked and abstract, in which the person who knows establishes a certain distance between himself and the affirmation of the truth. But there is also a fuller and clearer form of knowledge, the knowledge of the true and good which is born of an intimate affinity with the true and with the good, and a fundamental orientation of one's own person towards these values. If a man does not possess an elevated and genuine degree of goodness, he is forced to make somewhat greater efforts to arrive, only gradually, at a knowledge of moral values. A low moral level in the milieu about him makes it much more difficult for a man to arrive at a knowledge of the good and the true. The same thing happens in the case of knowledge of God.

Humanity as a whole, and each individual man within society, would have arrived at a much more full and spontaneous knowledge of the existence of God — even by the unaided powers of nature — if sin had not interferred with the normal progression of human history. The human family, as a whole, must not look for excuses if the knowledge of God has become more and more difficult for it. St. Paul tells us that "what can be known about God is plain, because God has shown it" (Rom. 1, 19). He obviously does not think that humanity had to wait for the rise and development of scientific philosophy to be perfectly and fully aware of the existence of God. "Ever since the creation of the world, his invisible nature, namely, his eternal power and deity, has been clearly perceived in the things that have been made" (Rom. 1, 20). Men — whether doctors in philosophy or all but uneducated — cannot supply any reasonable or rational justification for denying or casting doubt upon the existence of God. God reveals his wisdom and his goodness especially in the inner heart of man, whom he has created in "his image and likeness."

No Excuse

But since — beginning with our first parents — men have, in various ways, refused the recognition due to God, whom they should have learned to know on the basis of his works, the knowledge of God has grown pale and become confused and difficult for a large part of humanity. After all, how is it possible to rationally admit, in all truth, that "God has created us" if we are not willing to honor him as Lord and Creator? St. Paul explains this darkening of the human mind by the presence of sin, the ebb and flow of human sinfulness that has colored the whole of human history: "Although they knew God they did not honor him as God or give thanks to him, but they became futile in their thinking and their senseless minds were darkened. Claiming to be wise, they became fools" (Rom. 1, 21-22).

Karl Marx

These words are a description of the general case. They are not to be understood as a final judgment on the case of the individual person who might have arrived at full faith in God only by passing through great difficulties, inner struggles, and a long intellectual odyssey. The greatest difficulties frequently come from the unbelief in the world around us. Even more difficult may be the situation of the man who is faithful and quite sincere, living in a neighborhood that is statistically religious, regularly going to Church, but basically not too serious about his religion. Recall the enormous scandal that Karl Marx had to witness as a young man when his father, a Jew, had himself and his whole family baptized simply in order to encounter fewer obstacles in his social life, or the sad spectacle presented by the society world of that time in which religion was, at best, only an esthetic ornament. "They spoke of religion and were thinking of an opiate". His own impassioned denial of all religion is thus primarily, and more simply, only a denial of the religion of those who knew God but did not pay him the homage due to the Creator. God alone knows whether it was this impassioned revolt that made him sick and incapable of thinking about God in a reasonable and rational way.

Besides these difficulties which result from a practically atheistic or only externally religious milieu, there are also many other individual causes, psychological in nature, which make even an intelligent man and one inclined towards good, constantly feel the need to go back and re-weigh all the reasons for and against the existence of God.

Still, if we take the particular situation of a normal man living in a really Christian milieu and possessed of an exact knowledge of revelation, then it is evident that even the simple natural arguments, in the light of revelation, take on a much greater clarity, notwithstanding the fact of human sinfulness.

This is also the teaching of Vatican I, which, however, does not ignore or minimize the difficulties that sin puts in the way of knowing God: "As a result of this revelation, those things regarding God which are not inaccessible to human reason can be known by all men, with ease, with certainty, and without error, even in the present situation of the human race" (Denzinger 1786).

3

IS THE EXISTENCE OF GOD AS EVIDENT AS $2 + 2 = 4$?

I have arrived at the conviction that there are no rationally undeniable proofs for the existence of God, because if he had proposed the truth of his existence with the same logical force that underlies the proposition $2 + 2 = 4$, he would

*have practically destroyed the merit of our faith,
by obliging us to an unavoidable act of consent.*

It takes only a minimum of arithmetical skill to
understand that two and two are four. Even a mentally
retarded person, a schizophrenic for that matter, who is
incapable of a typically human decision, could still
follow the reasoning involved.

Demonstration and Proof

The question of the existence of God, on the other
hand, involves the whole man and his whole life. Thus,
it requires the cooperation of those human capacities
which are required for understanding a truth that is so
deep and marvelous. This is not to say that there are
no clear reasons which speak in favor of the existence
of God, nor, for that matter, that there are no reasons
which offer a greater degree of security to a more
enlightened mind.

But it is one thing to explain a mathematical truth
or a concept of natural science and quite another to
"demonstrate" the existence of God. The terms "demonstration and proof" take on a very particular meaning
in this last case, since we are no longer speaking on the
plane of natural science. No matter how hard they try,
chemistry, physics, astronomy, geology, or mathematics,
with the methodology and results of their scientific proce-
dures, cannot ever discover God, and the reason is a
simple one: God is not a particle of physical reality nor
an object of the laws that deal directly with physical

reality. Mathematical formulas could develop without the existence of God. The presence of God is not required to fill up any void or to complete any circle. Still, if the mathematician or the cultivator of natural science is not purely a technician locked up within his own discipline, but a man who asks himself the ultimate questions about the ultimate causes of reality, and experiences a sense of wonder in the face of the grand and marvelous, then he will necessarily feel himself bound to go beyond the limits of his science and ask himself the one ultimate and decisive question that every man has to ask himself: "What is the source of all these marvelous possibilities which science keeps discovering in the physical realities of this world?" In asking this question, he passes from scientist to philosopher: he becomes a "friend of wisdom." And every man is inevitably led to pose such a question as soon as he has acquired a certain degree of experience in living and a certain degree of knowledge about the world.

Whenever we pose the question of the existence of God, it is basically always man himself with whom we are preoccupied. The material world poses the question of its origin only in terms of the human person who can admire and use it or also abuse it. But even the sciences which are concerned directly with man, such as empirical psychology or sociology, are, in their turn, not in a position to demonstrate the existence of God in terms of their own proper methodology and within the framework of their own proper objects, even if they can give a much more immediate formulation to the problem of the ultimate foundation and the ultimate determinations that govern the individual person and human society. Even in this case, when we ask about God we have already gone beyond the framework of experimental psychology or sociology and become simply "men" who are, in the most authentic and profound sense of the word, friends of wisdom.

The problem of God's existence calls upon the most profound and the most sublime elements of our human potential, our thinking in all its range, our love, our aspirations. The more a person is a human being, the more he loves his neighbor and knows how to understand him, the more seriously he takes his own dignity, the more forcefully he is confronted by the problem of God, and the easier it is for him to understand that God has manifested himself in a clear and unmistakable manner, by means of his external works, as the source of all being and, what is more, as the archetype and creator of humanity.

Human Beings

In order to become a good practitioner of the natural sciences it is enough for a man to develop a determined capacity of the intellectual order. But to see clearly on the question of God's existence, a person has to be a human being in the fullest sense of the word; he needs to take his neighbor seriously; he needs to be honest and loyal in his attitude towards moral values.

The problem of human origins and the meaning of human existence, and the existence of other beings as well, is intimately bound up with certain clearly discernable spiritual truths which can be utilized as the basis of rigorously logical proofs, as, for example, when we demonstrate the necessary existence of an absolutely first cause in the world of reality, or when we attempt to establish a foundation and an ultimate meaning in the experience of consciousness. But when we touch such questions, it is, once again, the whole man who is involved, and the demonstrations lead to cogent conclusions only when they are embarked upon in a total manner; thus it is the whole human person with whom we must be preoccupied in this effort, with his whole human development, if we mean to arrive at a real knowledge of God's existence.

The Judgment of Credibility

With respect to the person and mission of Christ and the faith of the Catholic Church, history can offer some aid. But basically, even in this area, we are dealing with an inner spiritual eye, and an attitude towards both the person of Christ and the doctrine of the Church. With respect to the divinity of Christ, the word "demonstration" is less than accurate. The question goes like this: "Did Christ reveal himself in a sufficiently clear manner as the Son of the Eternal Father?" To answer this question, we need to have a total openness to truth and good, which, in Christ, are concretized in a living person. In order to have a reasonable faith, we have first to emit a judgment of credibility, which is to say that we must see whether the matter is worthy of being believed, as it actually is, in the case of Christ.

We must not forget that the true and proper act of faith also implies something far more precious: in this act, the Holy Spirit, sent by the Father and the Son, moves our own spirit, our heart, and our will, in such a manner that our assent achieves a much more lofty degree of fittingness and reasonability and imparts a sense of security and divine joy. In the last analysis, faith in Christ is a grace, a gift of God that is unmerited, a gift that is not granted to a blind man or a blinded man, but rather a gift that makes us clairvoyant, in a higher measure, for the more essential truths.

Human Warmth

When we want to communicate the treasure of faith to others, it is never enough to propose a series of rational arguments with the cold objectivity of the mathematician, or to employ the refined arts of psychology. Since it is a question of reawakening a human act in them, in the fullest sense of the word, we must approach them with the greatest respect for their human existence and make them feel warmth and nobility of human love.

As for faith in Christ, in whom the Father has revealed all his love, and as for faith in the Catholic Church, the Bride of Christ, Jesus himself, in his high-priestly prayer, has indicated the way: "That they may all be one; even as thou, Father, art in me, and I in thee, that they may also be in us, so that the world may believe that thou hast sent me" (John 17, 21).

Arriving at faith is not ever the result of a cold and objective process of demonstration, even if we are speaking of true knowledge, the highest and most sublime knowledge possible to man here below. In his prayer for the unity of his disciples as the way and medium of bringing all the world to believe in his mission, Jesus, according to the Gospel of St. John, first used the expression "that the world may *believe* that you have sent me" (17, 21), but immediately afterwards added "that the world may *know* that you have sent me" (17, 23). Between faith and knowledge there is not any contradiction, but only a marvelous unity, one which surpasses the exigencies of purely human powers, although it never completely excludes them.

4

CAN THE EXISTENCE OF GOD BE UNDERSTOOD, OR MUST IT SIMPLY BE BELIEVED?

Is the existence of God a truth that can be known by human intelligence without the aid of revelation, or must it be accepted by faith because God has revealed it? Where, in this area, does the human capacity to know through the unaided resources of human reason end, and where does the knowledge of faith begin? Must the existence of God and the divinity of Christ be treated on the same plane; that is, must they be accepted by faith, or is it possible for the existence of God to be accepted without recourse to faith? And

> *if the existence of God is not a truth of faith, but a truth that can be demonstrated by human reason, then is faith still possible? Where is the "merit of faith"?*

This question is fundamental in its importance, because it concerns a decisive area of religion, that is, the proper understanding of the act of faith. Faith begins when man opens himself to God, who speaks to him. When a person, by a deep and precise logical reasoning process, arrives at the conclusion that there must be a Supreme Being, possessed of all the perfection of being and existing as the first cause of everything else that is, he has obviously succeeded in arriving at one of the most sublime concepts. But this concept is not yet an act of religious faith. We can speak of faith only when a person goes beyond this logical observation and arrives at an understanding of the fact that this God has willed to manifest himself to *us*, to *me*, by means of his works, his creation, and his presence within my soul; I can recognize the fact of his existence because he has willed to manifest himself to me; thus he expects me to find him, to discover him within his works, to listen to him, and to place myself trustingly in his hands.

Religious Awareness

When, however, a person says that he is convinced, on the basis of his own reasoning, that there does exist a personal Supreme Being, but at the same time is of

the opinion that this God does not care about him and
does not expect any response on his part, then we are
in the presence of a person who, while he is not a one
hundred percent unbeliever, is still unreligious. Religion
demands a unity and a relationship with God. This
relationship, on the part of the man involved, requires
first of all a fundamental act that is the essence of faith;
faith in its turn is based on the fact that God himself
has willed this relationship and that he has manifested
himself to the intellect, heart, and will of man.

The act of faith which is supernatural and salutary
thus enters into the question only when a man's belief
is based not on the fact that God has willed to manifest
himself by means of his works, but on the fact that God
himself has moved him interiorly, by his grace, to
believe. This act is oriented towards God not as a
stranger — an "other" — but towards the true God who
is the *Thou* who speaks and answers to our *Ego*.

Faith in Christ

Faith in Christ, compared with general faith in the
existence of God, represents something new; the revelation of God in his dearly beloved Son is something new
and absolutely unheard of in the whole history of God's
self-revelation to man in the works of creation. The
life and activity of Jesus are an historical reality, even
though his divinity is a mystery that transcends all our
human wisdom. It is a perfectly reasonable thing, quite
in keeping with the sound laws of human logic, for a
man to believe in Christ, from the moment he has re-

vealed his divinity by means of the miracles he worked
and his whole life on earth. Still one can possibly emit
an act of faith in Christ without the special intervention
of God's grace. The act of faith is, thus, on the one hand,
perfectly reasonable, and, on the other hand, it immeas-
urably surpasses the potential of human reason: the act
of faith in Christ means accepting his own claim that
he is, for all men, the way, the truth, and the life.

Logic and Act of Faith

To sum up: the simple, logical, and well-reasoned
demonstration of the existence of God, or the simple
judgment of human reason that God does exist, are far
removed from the actual act of faith, which leads to
salvation. Under the influence of grace, of course, they
can be transformed into an act of faith which is distin-
guished primarily in terms of the following structure:
the principal object in view is the fact that God has
revealed himself; the assent to this fact is not the indif-
ferent judgment that is restricted to merely holding to
the truth that God exists; it consists in being open, in
abandoning oneself to him who has willed to reveal
himself to man; such faith in God always tends, of its
own innate nature, towards faith in Christ who is the
absolute and perfect revelation of God; it is only in
Christ that God has revealed the totality of his love
to man; face to face with Christ man too reveals what
is really within him, that is, whether or not he is really
open and receptive in the sight of God.

The question this reader asks ends up by calling

marked attention to the peculiar and individual characteristics of the act of faith. It is a complex and totalitarian act which calls upon the whole of man. The whole man is called upon to respond in the act of faith, and not only his intellect. In the case in which the believer is still living in sin, his act of faith obviously also implies a condemnation, in principle, of his sinfulness.

The Church

5

IS TRUTH TO BE FOUND ONLY IN THE CATHOLIC CHURCH?

In a fairly recent issue of the Famiglia Cristiana *I read an interview given by the well-known moral theologian, Fr. Bernard Häring. Among the questions he was asked I want to call attention to the following: "Is truth to be found only in the Catholic Church?" This was his answer: "The Catholic Church must not claim to possess a 'monopoly' on truth, since this would be contrary to Scripture. In the Bible we read that God created man in his own image and likeness, and that 'all' the heavens declare his marvels. Thus every man has preserved a part of the truth, and members of other religions have developed a fragment of the common fund of truth, perhaps in a more happy form than the Catholic Church."*

The answer is, no doubt, a very good one for someone who has a good understanding of the Bible or mystical theology. But for the ordinary reader — and Famiglia Cristiana *is read by millions of them — the context does not appear to be perfectly clear or easily intelligible. In fact, judging from what I have heard from many of the parishioners, the answer is actually a little disturbing.*

The same question has been asked by the Second Vatican Council, in its decree on ecumenism. Are we the only ones who possess the truth? Do the other Christian sects teach only error and deception? Every word in the Council's pronouncement reflects the humble and joyous gratitude of the Catholic Church which alone can claim to be the true Church of Christ. But this does not make her blind to the good and truth that is to be found in the other Christian communities or even in the religions which are not Christian.

Only the Church is Infallible

The Church is the only religious society which has received the divine promise: "The gates of hell will not prevail against you." Only the Catholic Church enjoys an infallible magisterium, capable of making decisions which bear the absolute guarantee of truth. Still, it is this truth itself which obligates the Church to distinguish

accurately between what she teaches with the guarantee
of absolute infallibility and those many other areas in
which she points out the way of salvation, without formu-
lating any definitive decisions. She also teaches, in a
very exact way, whatever is necessary for salvation; but
she does not have an answer that is ready, absolutely
secure, and really binding for every question.

Even in the important points of faith there is a certain
development, a slow and gradual growth, a successive
clarification. We need only recall the development of
the doctrine on the Blessed Mother. In 1300, as brilliant
and holy a theologian as St. Thomas Aquinas still doubted
whether the Blessed Mother had been conceived without
original sin from the very first moment of her existence.
It is true that God's revelation to man has closed with
the death of the Apostles, but the consequences that this
foundation implies becomes clear only with the passage
of centuries. That is why the Church will continue to
explain the truths of salvation in a better and better
developed form, until the very day of Christ's return,
giving each truth the position and importance it deserves.

In some areas, certain truths have been lost sight of
for a certain period of time, or have been completely
neglected. A large portion of the faithful may pay
particular attention to some individual truths, for a long
period of time, or practice certain secondary forms of
spirituality at the expense of neglecting other more
fundamental ones.

The debates carried on in the course of the Council
at St. Peter's have clearly shown that what the Church
bears within herself is always the common treasure and

deposit of the faith. At the same time the discussion has revealed the fact that the Church cannot permit herself a lazy and complacent sense of security. She is on the right road to salvation, but the people of God always remains on pilgrimage here below, seeking its way towards the one true fatherland.

Good and Truth are to be Found Everywhere

Humility, love of truth, and, above all, the honor of God oblige the Church to recognize the beauty and good that God has created and continues to create and produce even in those men who are not her members. Many theologians think that in the damned, in hell, there is no longer even a bit of good to be found; but no Catholic theologian would dare to maintain that those who have not yet attained the fulness of faith, that is, the Christian communities separated from Rome, do not have anything to offer in the way of truth and goodness. The Decree on Ecumenism lists several important truths that the various non-Catholic churches have preserved together with the Catholic Church. And Pope Paul VI, at the beginning of the second session of the Council, made the statement that not only do they preserve these truths, but they have also developed them in a useful and propitious manner. We need think only of the traditional and profound esteem in which the liturgy has always been held among the Orientals, even after their separation from Rome, or the profound attachment and faith in the Scriptures that is characteristic of so many Protestant sects.

The Catholic Church is the "support and foundation of truth" (I Tim. 3, 15), but by this very fact it has a duty to appreciate the truth — wherever it is to be found. It has no cause to be jealous when it discovers the wonderful ways in which God, in his goodness, is at work even in those who are not its members, keeping alive the bonds that join them to Catholic truth and laying the foundation for their eventual unity with Rome.

6

THE CHURCH AND PROGRESS

It was with obvious disappointment that I read how, in December of 1864, the then Pope, Pius IX, published a Syllabus in which, among other things, he maintained (and I quote): "The Roman Pontiff neither can nor ought to reconcile himself with progress, with liberalism, and with modern society." This is fine, as far as I am concerned, with respect to liberalism; but the rest of it is quite beyond my grasp. Could you please explain it?

The last proposition of the Syllabus, number 80, does not actually say that the Roman Pontiff neither can nor ought to reconcile himself with progress, liberalism, and modern society. It is rather the opposite formulation that is condemned: "The Roman Pontiff can and ought to become reconciled and enter into agreement with progress, with liberalism, and with modern society."

And, in fact, there were more than sufficient reasons for being opposed to a proposition formulated in such a vague and generic manner. Among other things, many people thought that the Pope should, in the name of true freedom, genuine culture, and authentic progress, approve of everything that was then being so highly lauded as progress, as liberalism, and as modern society. But this he could not do, because not everything about these movements was true and genuine progress.

We need think only of the absurd nationalism of those years, and those theses of liberalism which opened the door to indifferentism in the face of truth, or refused, as a matter of principle, to recognize the existence of absolute and binding truths.

From the point of view of theory and doctrine, the condemnation of this proposition is, accordingly, perfectly proper, and it was deservedly introduced into the Syllabus. In condemning it, Pius IX is guilty of neither oversight nor error.

Church and Progress

Today, in the era of the Second Vatican Council, and in the spirit of Pope John, there is no doubt that we would be inclined to prefer a more pastoral and optimistic formulation of the same truth. It is, in my opinion, very important for us to keep this in mind in our lay apostolate. The actual meaning of proposition 80 of the Syllabus could, for example, be expressed more or less in these terms:

1. The Church is happy to recognize progress in every field; but first it is necessary to ask, with all seriousness, what progress really is. All too often, the name progress is mistakenly applied to what is actually a step backwards and an insult to the dignity of man.

2. The Church realizes that her vocation in the world is to be the bulwark and courageous defender of freedom. Her whole preoccupation in this respect is to insure the fact that man can develop his freedom, in as perfect a manner as possible, by using the good things that God has given him. The Church thus proposes full freedom even in accepting the Gospel and the Faith, and, on the other hand, positively rejects any form of violence or discrimination in dealing with non-Catholics. She cannot, however, subscribe to any form of liberalism that proceeds from basic indifferentism in the face of truth.

3. The Church is not bound to any particular form of culture or government. She recognizes and accepts, quite willingly, everything that is good in modern society. But, for the good of human society and the good of the state itself, she also clearly points out how much is wrong and false, and thus how much needs to be improved.

The Bible

7

THE REAL MEANING OF GENESIS

In Genesis, we can find statements which are contrary to common sense, if nothing else. There we read, for example, that the Supreme Being made Adam, and then from one of Adam's ribs made Eve, and then, in the course of time, these two first parents gave birth to Cain first, and then Abel and Japheth (sic). Cain, as we know, killed Abel, etc., etc. So far we have read of only these few persons. Then one day Cain decides to take a wife; so he sets out for a neighboring country (note these words, now, "neighboring country"), takes a wife, and founds the city of Enoch. Japheth, following his brother's example, goes to some country or other and also takes a wife. How are we to explain the exist-

*ence of these other nations in the world at that
time?*

The question is interesting in more than one respect.
Among other things, it shows that the *Famiglia Cristiana*
is read by some persons who are faced with a serious
crisis of faith which they cannot succeed in simply
dismissing from their minds. Even though the question,
the way it is asked, at first glance does appear to be
somewhat blunt and insulting, I firmly believe that the
person who asks it would like to be able to believe with
all his heart. Should he perhaps be reproved for having
dared to manifest his ignorance of these affairs before
such a wide circle of readers? Or perhaps we ourselves
are partially at fault for this ignorance of the explanations which the Church supplies to such questions.
Those priests (and those laymen) are at fault who have
not seriously studied the arguments in question, and
when they are asked about such questions, give a simple
and poorly thought out answer that would dissatisfy any
thinking man in our twentieth century.

Then we must also recall the great scandal caused,
in recent years, by certain members of the clergy and
certain Catholic theologians, champions of orthodoxy,
who have secretly or openly opposed the Encyclical of
Pius XII on the Bible, *Divino afflante Spiritu.* The gross
ignorance exhibited in this question is nothing compared
to the ignorance of certain people in the Church, fond
of argument and debate, who, fortunately, are few in
number and seldom taken seriously by the Catholic
world as a whole. The crusade they have inaugurated

revolves primarily about the so-called "method of form criticism" as applied to the study of the Bible, or — what amounts to practically the same thing — the explicit invitation of Pius XII to investigate, and take into account, in explaining and interpreting the Bible, the literary form used by the authors of the individual books, since only in this way is it possible to understand what they intended to say and teach.

Understanding the Bible

This group of theologians has, obviously, not gone so far as to assume the position of some religious sects who do not think it is even necessary to refer to the original text of the Bible, and who, without bothering to study anything of the original languages or manner of thinking and forms of expression proper to the times in which the Bible was written, to say nothing of the cultural milieu in which it was composed, read the Bible as if it had been written in English, according to the mentality and style of our own century. If they were affected by a serious case of mental sloth, they could hardly have managed to take such a determined stand against the directives of Pius XII and the whole of modern Catholic Biblical science. The opponents of Pius XII — perhaps they were too busy doing other things — have not sufficiently examined the history of the Catholic Church and the cultural background of the inspired authors of Sacred Scripture.

St. Augustine, before he arrived in Milan faced precisely the same difficulties with the literal meaning of the Old Testament as those faced by the man who asked our question today. He was, indeed, a mighty professor of rhetoric, but his opinions on the subject of Sacred Scripture were only personal and very superficial, for the most part opinions arrived at by the opponents of the Catholic Church, and formed on the basis of his very fragmentary and bird's-eye scanning of the text of Scripture. But when he arrived at Milan and listened to the explanations of the saintly Bishop Ambrose, explanations which were called "allegorical" at that time, all his difficulties simply vanished. It was then he realized that a proper understanding of the meaning of the authors of the sacred books was the only key to solving all the questions and problems that were plaguing him. Not only that, but, being a fair and open-minded man, he also realized that certain problems regarding the precise meaning of certain biblical texts were an open question which could be freely discussed.

St. Augustine Before and After

Upon returning to Africa as a Catholic Bishop, a man of open and even child-like faith but at the same time a very sharp and demanding logician, he wrote a commentary on the Book of Genesis that deserves to be called really modern in many respects. In this book he assembles the explanations already developed before his time by the theological schools of Alexandria in Egypt and Antioch in Syria. He managed to achieve a clear appreciation of the broader outlines of the problem that is posed by modern Biblical science today, when it speaks of the "history of literary forms," or the "literary genre," that is, the problem of understanding the mode of expression that the author of a given book has used, and how this literary genre was understood by his contemporaries, a mode of expression and interpretation which are not always clear and obvious to us today, considering the different cultural background in which we live. In other words, the problem consists in determining what is the religious truth that the author intends to communicate to his contemporaries in a style and manner that is comprehensible to them. What he really meant to say, and really said, in a manner intelligible to his contemporaries, is what is infallibly true in Scripture.

The inspired author of the story of Adam and his posterity is not so naive as the superficial reader of today might first be inclined to believe. Just like the modern man of today, he fully realized that the first offspring of the first human couple could not just that simply find another tribe, or have so many children that he could found a city all by himself.

Not a Naive Account

But what does the author of Genesis mean to recount in this narrative, in this mode of expression that he chose as being well adapted to his contemporaries? He means simply to affirm that the first human couple was created immediately by God, without being concerned about whether or not God's creative activity passed through a long and gradual process of evolution of life leading up to the moment in which he immediately breathed the soul of life into the human body, or whether he created man by immediately forming his body, too, from inorganic material, without any prior course of evolution. What he means to stress in the account is this: man owes his existence totally and solely to the love of his Creator God, and he is completely dependent on him. Beyond that, the author also means to teach that our first parents did not successfully pass the test that God imposed upon them, and seriously offended the God who had created them in his love.

Interpreting the Story

The story of Cain down to Lamech (Gen. 4, 1-23) clearly shows, in a grandiose interpretation of human history, how the original sin of our first parents led to a rapidly expanding growth of personal sin in their descendants. Cain is the prototype of the man who hates, the fratricide, while another insert into the history (Gen. 4, 17) stresses the multiplication of sin and vice in the urban culture that was beginning to develop. Original sin makes its consequences felt primarily in the personal sins of Adam's seed, who all take on a certain similarity with the prototype Cain.

On the other hand, in the rural culture of those times, with respect to the growing effects of the curse of sin, the inspired author depicts a rather elevated state of morality, as represented in the person of Abel, and especially Seth, whose offspring honored and feared God and "called upon the name of the Lord" (Gen. 4, 26).

The influence of sin in the descendants of Cain is

described in a dramatic manner. Lamech inaugurates polygamy, is a violent braggart, and proves himself to be much more vindictive than his predecessors.

Everything points to the fact that the inspired author is not concerned with narrating the precise history, complete with names and dates, of Adam's offspring. A reader who has learned to recognize the literary genres of the Hebrew language will not suppose that the author intends to locate the precise position Lamech occupies in the line of Adam's descendants. What he is concerned with and what he means to call particular attention to is the personification of certain historical phenomena in that name, phenomena which are the result of original sin and so much personal sin, especially polygamy, hate, vengeance, and murder.

8

DOES THE BIBLE FORBID STATUES?

The Bible says: "Thou shalt not make any sculp-
ture or graven image of anything that is in
heaven or on earth or in the water under the
earth.

Thou shalt not adore such things nor serve
them, etc." Now what I want to know is this:

(1) Has Christ abrogated this prohibition against
making statues and images? (2) Is there any

*passage in the New Testament that expressly
contains this abrogation?*

Are the Ten Commandments still valid? Can the
Church, in proposing her formularies for examining our
conscience, simply omit or overlook one of these precepts?

These are questions of great importance, because they
reveal the existence of a serious danger in Christian
thinking, the danger that, in forming his conscience, the
Christian remains anchored in the thinking and climate
of the Old Testament and refuses to pass over to the New.

The Christian must form his conscience in the light
of the new laws promulgated by Christ; these are pro-
claimed primarily in the Sermon on the Mount (St. Mat-
thew's Gospel, ch. 5 ff.) and in the Farewell Discourse
(Gospel of St. John, ch. 14 ff.). The Second Vatican
Council wants to impress all Christians everywhere with
the truth of the fact that our Savior's words: "Be perfect
just as your Father in heaven is perfect" (Matt. 5, 48),
and "This is my commandment, that you love one another
as I have loved you" (John 15, 12) are a precept binding
upon all our Savior's disciples, a precept that points out
the constant direction of the path we need to walk in
imitating him.

Old and New Law

The man who clings solely to the Ten Commandments
of the Old Testament shows that he is not really in
heartfelt agreement with the good news of the Gospel,

that he either does not know, or does not properly appreciate, the freedom of God's law of grace. The Ten Commandments were promulgated on Mount Sinai, amid thunder and lightning, to a people who were hard of heart. The new Law is the glad message promulgated on the Mount of the Beatitudes, and in the intimate atmosphere of the Last Supper, never losing sight of the Cross and Resurrection. Anyone who remains conscious and aware of these magnificent manifestations of Christ's love cannot help feeling drawn to a new vocation, living his whole life under the law of faith and gratitude: "How can I give thanks to the Lord, for all the gifts he has given me?" (Ps. 115, 3).

This, however, does not mean that we can be content with making a less generous response to the clear demands of the Decalogue. The Christian has an obligation to do more, and he does it with real joy when he is really filled with faith in the joyful news of the Gospel.

Two precepts of the Ten Commandments have been abolished in the New Testament, or, to put it better, have been perfected in a sublime manner: The Christian does not observe the Sabbath as a simple day of rest. In its place he makes a feast day of the first day of the week, the *Dies Dominicus,* the Lord's Day, and not simply by resting from his labor, as in the former Sabbath observance, but by including in it the even more noble activity of adoring God and celebrating the holy mysteries. The earliest Church Councils all taught that Christians are not bound to observe the Sabbath precept, and that they should regard the Lord's Day as something more than a mere substitute for the Sabbath.

Reasons behind the Prohibition

The same thing is true regarding the prohibition against making statues. Because of the pagan atmosphere which surrounded them and the hardness of their hearts, the Hebrews were in constant danger of giving in to the temptation to adore statues. That is why our Lord forbade them to make statues. But in Jesus Christ, God has revealed the perfect image of his invisible glory, and we must adore him as true God. The Second Council of Nicea, which condemned the Iconoclasts, taught that we "must confess Christ as the perfect handwriting of God, in his humanity." In the same way we can also see a visible message of God in the saints, and their statues become a sort of handwriting that everyone can read. The Fourth Council of Constantinople and the Council of Trent have, each in its turn, solemnly defined the Church's right to depict statues and images and use them properly for the adoration of God and the veneration of the saints.

Just as the proper observance of Sunday in Christian worship perfects and surpasses, essentially, the Sabbath precept, the same thing is true of the veneration of statues; no Christian could possibly think of adoring statues as such, and thus there is no longer any prohibition against making pictures and statues of God and the saints.

Sacred Scripture contains all the necessary teachings on this subject, and the Church, faithful to her living tradition, needs only to draw the logical consequences for Christian life.

9

HAS HITLER REHABILITATED THE JEWS IN THE SIGHT OF GOD?

Some time ago I was reading about the guilt the Jews incurred in the crucifixion of Christ. Now, I would like to know whether the expiation suffered by the Jewish people during the Second World War has rehabilitated the Jews, in the sight of divine justice, from the guilt they incurred in putting Christ to death.

It is unjust to charge all the Jews of Christ's day, as a unit, or the Jews of today, with the guilt of deicide. It was only a few hundred, or, at most, a few thousand, who cried: "Crucify him!" while the others all followed his teaching from the very beginning.

Actually, the responsibility for Christ's death, the death that expiated for the sins of all mankind, rests with our own sins no less than those of the Jews of those days and today.

On the other hand, we too can all take part in the expiatory death of Christ by our willingness to accept the suffering that enters into our life, by performing works of penance, by patiently bearing with the tribulations of our state in life. This does not exclude the Jews, all the Jews who have suffered so much; they too, by accepting death in a spirit of resignation to God's will, have cooperated in the expiatory death of Christ;

they too, by bearing with persecution and death in the hope and expectation of salvation, have helped to expiate for "our" sins.

Terror of Genocide

Hitler, in attempting to exterminate the Jews, was certainly not carrying out any divine mission; he was simply commiting a terrible sin against the commandments of God. God permitted this evil. And we must suppose that he supplied the poor victims with sufficient grace to keep from cursing God or losing faith in him, faced with the terrifying fate that awaited them, and that they had sufficient grace to bear with everything in the spirit of religion.

Still it is impossible to claim that Hitler has rehabilitated the Jews in the sight of God. We can, however, confidently hope that, in the plans of Providence, the indescribable sufferings of the Jews have proved to be fruitful for salvation, for our salvation, and primarily for that of the Jews themselves.

To the very end of time, God will always have compassion on the nation that was once his chosen people. Many, very many of them have certainly found the road to salvation by virtue of their good faith and earnest expectation of the Redeemer.

Our task today as Christians is clear; we have an obligation to show the Jewish people, and every individual Jew we meet in our daily life, the love and respect that will enable them to realize that the Redeemer has established the reign of his love on earth.

It is not the massacres of Hitler, but our Christian love, that can and must fully rehabilitate the Jews in our world today. The testimony of our faith and love — in the splendid example of Pope John — will eventually succeed in opening, even for this tortured people, the door of God's great kingdom.

Christian Morality

10

MARRIAGE AND VIRGINITY

In what sense is virginity superior to marriage?

Thanks to God, our days have seen a truly wonderful development in the doctrine on marriage as the great road to holiness and sanctification. The associations of married people, dedicated to personal sanctification and the work of the lay apostolate, have all the semblance of a modern religious congregation. We need think only of the Christian Family Movement, in the United States and Canada, which numbers more than 45,000 families, all working in the same spirit to increase the depth of their own faith and to perfect the working methods of their apostolic activity. Does any of this prejudice the ideals of virginity and religious life? Not at all.

Respect and esteem for virginity presupposes respect and esteem for Christian marriage, for many reasons. The greater the number of saintly married people, the

more numerous and better prepared will be the vocations
to the priesthood and religious life. The Council of
Trent solemnly teaches that anyone who asserts that the
married state is to be preferred to the state of virginity
or celibacy, or teaches that it is not better to remain
in a state of virginity or celibacy than it is to marry, is
to be excommunicated (Denz. 980). These words,
at the very same time, clearly teach that the married
state is something good and a way of life blessed by God.
If we look down upon the value and importance of
marriage, then the Council's statement on virginity as
a "better" state has lost much of its meaning. The flourishing of a matrimonial spirituality is thus a prerequisite
for a proper appreciation of the higher state of virginity.

The Church does not teach that those who live in
the state of virginity are better than those who live a
married life. The comparison affects only the two walks
of life taken in themselves. For the individual person,
the only essential thing is to discover, and fulfill, the
way of life to which God has called him. Not all men
are called to virginity. To attempt such a walk of life
without being interiorly called to it would involve the
risk of losing one's immortal soul. And those who feel
such an interior call must ascribe it to the grace of God
and follow his invitation conscientiously and with humility.

Vocation to Virginity

But precisely why is the state of virginity "better
and more blessed"? It is impossible to touch upon all

the pertinent reasons, or even enumerate all the more important elements recognized by the Church. But we must mention a few. The call to virginity is a free gift of God's love, a whole chain of graces that produce that freedom of spirit within the chosen soul which makes it possible for him to renounce married love for the love of the kingdom of heaven. The state of virginity is a joyous testimony to the fulness of grace in the present era of salvation, grace which makes it possible to have a full, joyous, and undivided love for Christ, and a spirit and heart that are on fire with zeal for the salvation of souls. Marriage and family life require and make possible a great and intimate love between husband and wife, between parents and children. The state of virginity implies undivided service and is interested love for all men, without distinction, in the measure in which they have a need for kindness and love. Marriage is a sacrament, symbolizing the eternal pact of love between Christ and his Church; it shares this love in a transitory form and measure. Virginity, on the other hand, is the proclamation and incarnation of the love that does not pass away, and thus it is an even more eloquent testimony to the eternal pact of love between Christ and his Church. The married state thus inevitably involves the temptation to be too exclusively concerned with things that pass away, even if the grace of the sacrament does, of itself, confer the grace to overcome the temptation. Virginity, too, has its temptations, but still it proclaims, clearly and intelligibly, to all men, that "the form of this world is passing away" (I Cor.

7, 31); by this very fact it is a constant admonition, not only for those who have embraced it, but for all Christians everywhere, to search tirelessly for the things that abide for all eternity — love of God and the disinterested love of neighbor.

The greater blessedness of the state of virginity consists in its intimate and undivided friendship with our Lord, which permit us to love in union with him, and to do the maximum amount of good for the greatest number of people, making it possible for them too to share the love of Christ. On the other hand, it also implies a very high degree of renunciation to very worth-while human value; it demands the spirit of poverty and many sacrifices, because it is a gift we carry in a vessel of clay. This renunciation, and these sacrifices, united with the sacrifice of Christ, are not an insignificant contribution to the effort of supporting the burden of married people in their many sacrifices and constant temptations against the virtue of married chastity. The state of virginity is thus a living sacrifice of praise in union with the Risen Christ, who dispenses the Holy Spirit with such fulness, and who, in the victory of love and freedom of the virgin sons of God, recalls the promise of the resurrection and happiness that is to be.

11

HOW ARE WE TO SPEAK OF THE PROBLEMS OF MARRIED LIFE?

One day when I was listening to a sermon, I heard the priest say, in explaining the sixth commandment, that matters relating to this commandment did not need to be explained to true Christians. I firmly disagree with this. Today it must be discussed more than ever before. There are too many engaged people, particularly young ladies, who have a false sense of shame, and who are actually afraid of their own fiancés, young ladies who grow strangely ashamed and silent whenever the subject of conversation turns to the impending birth of a new baby, in the marriage they are about to enter. This should not be so; it is important to give advice to engaged couples and explain what the Church thinks and feels about the subject of procreation. Marriage cannot be expected to succeed unless there is clear understanding on these points.

Today all the loudspeakers of the world — movies, television, newspapers and magazines — discourse freely on the intimate details of married life. On the train, at work, along the street — everywhere people talk quite openly about it. All too frequently the subject is discussed in a tone and manner that make it impossible for anyone who preserves even the least trace of modesty and decency to listen without blushing or being ill at ease. Faced with such language, which should never be found on the lips of a true Christian, many people, even priests, are, as a consequence, inclined to be overly reticent on the subject of intimate married life.

This, of course, is an erroneous conclusion. When we hear Mass or confession or the other sacraments made fun of, are we supposed to keep quiet? Must we never again mention God or the great mysteries of religion? Quite the contrary. We should take such opportunities as an occasion to teach others to speak properly, and with the necessary reverence, about religious matters. Thus the whole conversation gives greater glory to God and edification to our neighbor. We also beg and implore God for the grace to teach other people to speak in such a way as to make foolish people hold their tongues, and to teach them, effectively, to use language that is both correct and Christian.

It sometimes seems that it was the devil himself who invented the vocabulary for expressing the most intimate marital relationships. The Cathari, an heretical sect of the Middle Ages who have had a considerable influence on many parts of Italy and France, regarded sex life as the principle of all evil, and could not believe that it was the work of a good and just God.

Sacred Scripture, however, teaches something quite different. Scripture speaks of the love between engaged and married people. Think of the Song of Songs, where God speaks in imagery of the love he has for his chosen people, comparing it to the love that exists between bride and groom. Genesis, the first book of the Bible, describes the joy and gratitude of Adam when God presents him with the first woman, Eve, and puts into his mouth the inspired words that Christ himself and St. Paul later quote: "This is why a man will leave father and mother and cling to his wife and they will be one flesh" (2, 14). Adam and Eve felt no uneasiness; they were extremely free in their relationship. It is true that after their fall the situation changed; after that time not even husband and wife can freely and naturally find the proper and dignified words they need to speak of their love and their mission as married people. Even after original sins, however, married love and marriage relations remain something good, the work of the Creator, redeemed by Christ and raised to the unheard of dignity of a sacrament.

Dialogue between the Children of God

The sacrament of marriage is not, after all, something extrinsic, something added to the externals of conjugal love, as if it were simply an outside help and an actual grace, no matter how sanctifying it proves to be, no matter how much it helps to transform conjugal love itself, in its orientation towards procreation and fecundity. As a result, we can, and must, speak of matrimony as a sacrament, and everything that concerns conjugal love, with the same sense of wonder and the same respect with which we speak of baptism and confession.

The Bible says that Adam "knew" Eve, his wife. This term was used to refer to conjugal love, even in its most intimate respects, and it serves to demonstrate that such love is not simply a matter of instinct or something animal. It is a physical expression, employing the activity of the human body, of the spiritual personality; it is an act of mutual recognition, a word, a dialogue. Its language and terminology must be that of the redeemed children of God, a mutual self-giving in mutual happiness and joy, and husband and wife must look upon it as a presentiment of the love of God: "How wonderful, how ecstatic must the love of God prove to be, if love between two human creatures can be so blessed and so wonderful."

Language of Sin

If the Christian husband and wife do not make an effort to create a marriage vocabulary that is steeped in faith and prayer, it is obvious that the only vocabulary left to fill the purpose is the language coined by sin. If husband and wife do not learn to discuss such matters in the light of God, their married life will never experience the liberating influence and benefit of a dialogue that is genuinely human and Christian, and their most intimate relationships will never rise to the plane of the spiritual, never be transfigured into the dignity of human dialogue. Husband and wife have an obligation to discuss their difficulties, and shortcomings in this domain with all humility and in a spirit or repentance before God, with the intention of the helping, forgiving, and mutually understanding each other. The Christian dialogue of faith and humility produces a liberating and purifying strength.

It is obvious that engaged people cannot permit themselves these discussions on the more intimate aspects of married life and married love (discussions which might well be obligatory for husband and wife) simply because they are not yet joined by the indissoluble bond of matrimony. Still, they too must learn to speak properly of their future mission in life. The achievement of a truly chaste, modest, and respectful dialogue on these subjects will not permit the development of an unhealthy atmosphere; it will protect them from the danger of crude and improper temptations, just as the sun dissipates the clouds.

The young seminarian, as he advances step by step in his training for the ministry, achieves an ever clearer understanding of the meaning of the priestly powers of celebrating Mass and forgiving sins, but he would not think of using these powers before he is ordained a priest. In the same way, engaged couples who are taking their marriage instructions and discussing their future roles in the light of faith and with proper reverence are forearming themselves against the temptation of attempting the enjoyment, prior to their marriage vows, of what is the exclusive privilege and right of matrimony.

12

FAITHFULNESS WITHOUT LOVE?

Whenever the problem of marital infidelity is discussed, it is always in terms of a betrayal of married love. In my case — at 22 I made the tragic mistake of confusing love with a passing infatuation and attempted to raise a family on the result — does it make any sense to speak of a betrayal? What sense does it make for me to be faithful to a wife I do not really love?

Infidelity in marriage is always a betrayal of conjugal love. This is true even if, at the moment that the marriage was first contracted, there was no real understanding of the depth and scope of Christ's love, which is supposed to be mirrored in the constancy of conjugal love.

When we say that marriage is a bond of love, we do not mean to say, first of all, in theological terms, that we are speaking of a bond that is based on a romantic or sentimental love. Marriage was a bond of love even in those days in which parents used to pick out a wife for their son, and it was the duty of the head of the family, primarily, to see to the proper choosing of a mate for his children. If they were wise and proper parents, they were primarily concerned with making their children happy and, to that end, they realized that a marriage could be happy and successful only if husband and wife loved each other faithfully.

Bond of Love

But when we say that marriage, insofar as it is a bond of love, demands unconditioned fidelity, this is in consideration of an even more profound truth. It is, ultimately, a question of holding fast to God's own plans. It is he who first established marriage as a bond of love. Husband and wife are destined to be a witness to their paternal and maternal love for their children, and a witness to each other first of all, by mutually helping one another to arrive at a more fully vital awareness of their calling. How great a happiness must flow from the love of God, if the mutual love of husband and wife is already so rich in blessing and joy. The bond of fidelity between God and his Church is a bond of love, and God proves himself faithful, even when his chosen people are not faithful at all. The people of God lives in the merciful fidelity of God and knows, thereby, that it is bound to a like fidelity.

The marriage vow, spoken at the altar, is more than a simple affirmation of reciprocal love. It is a sacred oath, expressing the marriage partners' voluntary assent to the terms of marriage as a sacred bond of love. This means that they oblige themselves to grow in love and to purify their mutual love of everything that is unworthy and incorrect. Only a fool could think of undertaking marriage without understanding what is involved, or building his whole future life on the basis of a passing infatuation.

The atheistic world of today still uses all the solemn protestations of love that date from an era in which people believed strongly in the faithful love of God. For our modern, secularistic world, a marriage of love is merely an experiment that can always be called off by either of the contracting parties: once the passion and infatuation that first passed for the signs of true love have vanished, once there is no longer any mutual advantage to be gained, the marriage vow is disregarded.

For the believing Christian, marriage is a contract entered into in fidelity to the great plan of God who designed marriage as the image and type of his own faithful and merciful love. God loves us just as we are, in order to transform us into what he wants us to become.

It is precisely when the first infatuation has worn off in marriage that the Christian must show his faith in God's plan, that he must once more learn to love his God as a Person and welcome all the opportunities he has to prove this love in terms of his daily living. On the basis of this purified vision of married love, the Christian must once more learn to be more affectionate towards his marriage partner, and give a more profound meaning to their most intimate physical and moral union. A decisive and generous acceptance of God's plan, together with mutual prayer, can reawaken the true dimensions of married life, a fuller and richer existence, a more affectionate and deeper married, Christian love.

13

IS THE COMMAND TO "INCREASE AND MULTIPLY" ALWAYS BINDING WITH THE SAME URGENCY IN EVERY AGE?

In considering the "primary end" of marriage as the procreation and education of offspring, the Catholic position is based on the verse from Genesis: "Increase and multiply and fill the earth" (1, 28; 9, 1). To people the earth in a responsible way or to fill it up? In order to understand this command more accurately, it would be interesting to know the original text, as it is written in Hebrew. It might also be useful to recall that this exhortation, made by Yahweh to the wise man Noah, dates back to the days of the flood, some 45 centuries ago, when it was certainly justifiable, since the whole earth after the deluge, for want of men to inhabit it, must have looked like one big cemetery. But how can it possibly be defended today, when a Pontiff like Paul VI, faced with the serious problems of a population explosion, is paternally concerned with discovering a "natural means" to achieve the blessing of "responsible parenthood"? It does no good to look for an answer in the Gospel, since Christ, who loved children so much and pointed to them as examples of innocence, never preached an

*increase in the natural birth rate without also
exalting the merits of chastity.*

No one can say, with any degree of certainty, exactly
when the commandment about "increasing and multi-
plying" was actually formulated. It is merely a theological explanation of God's purpose in creation, and its
exactness is guaranteed by the fact of inspiration, precisely in the sense in which the inspired author wanted it
to be understood.

In my opinion, it is impossible to maintain that this
passage is to be taken as a confirmation of the fact that
God has created man and woman as the only possible
way to multiply the human race; God could have also
created a different method of achieving this same purpose. Nor does the passage in question mean to say
that the multiplication of the human race is the primary
purpose intended by God, such that every other purpose
is merely secondary in importance. In a word: I maintain that the multiplication and spread of the human race
is not a matter of secondary importance in God's plan,
or a matter of merely secondary importance in fulfilling
the purpose of marriage. It is a calling of the highest
sublimity. On the other hand, however, it does not
seem proper to use the term "secondary purpose" of
God's plan in speaking of an element of marriage that
is mentioned in the same context (Gen. 2, 14-24), that is,
the meaning and purpose of human bisexuality, or, to
put it more precisely, the meaning and purpose of
marriage and conjugal love. The Bible text does not
furnish any grounds for distinguishing between the

primary and secondary purposes in God's plans with respect to marriage.

Two Essential Lights

From what the Second Vatican Council has said on the subject of marriage it seems evident that the Church does not consider conjugal love as a secondary element, just as she does not think of the sublime vocation of husband and wife to cooperate with the creative love of God and to educate their children as something secondary and marginal — for she considers children as the heirs of eternal life. The inspired author of Genesis, in a grandiose and harmonious vision (1, 28), clearly shows how noble and how divinely blessed the vocation of mother and father really is. "God blessed them and said to them: Increase and multiply and fill the earth." Then, in the second chapter (14-24), he mentions an equally great gift in the fact of conjugal love. It is God himself who led Eve to Adam. She is God's great gift to the man, and Adam is filled with joy when he beholds her. She is the one creature who perfectly complements and corresponds to his nature, in its most intimate depths. Once God has led them together, they belong to each other in an indissoluble marriage and in a faithful love.

Genuine conjugal love and the vocation of procreating and educating children are not two separate or parallel ends of marriage. True married love is the source from which springs this desire for children, the source from which the parents derive the strength they need to love and care for them properly. When husband

and wife want children, they do not think in terms of "filling the earth." They are not motivated primarily by a consideration of political demography, nor is this what the inspired author of Genesis meant to inculcate. The words "fill the earth" are only meant to indicate the fact that God wants the human race to multiply in a marvelously prolific way, by means of the blessing and duty he has entrusted to married people.

Responsible Parenthood

This text, as translated above, is a good enough rendering of the essential elements of the original Hebrew. Thus it is not really possible to discover, in the text quoted, any particular connection with the situation which obtained right after the great flood. On the other hand, we must also admit, and never forget the fact, that these words carried an urgency, and signified a command that were much more impelling for humanity of old which was threatened on all sides by so much disease, epidemic, pestilence, dangers of every kind, and a much higher infant mortality rate. If, on the other hand, a particular region is already overdeveloped, such that it becomes rather difficult to find a position or a job for one's children in the society in which one lives, then these facts also need to be reflected in an attitude of responsible parenthood, such as is authoritatively recognized and recommended in the Pastoral Constitution on the Church in the Modern World, as published by the recent Council. Actually, there is still a good deal of room left on the earth. But, in the last analysis, when good Christian parents courageously bring a child into this world, it is not his social or economic position in life that they are thinking of or worried about; what they want to find for him is a place, together with them, in the eternal home, the heavenly Jerusalem. The ultimate and decisive reality in God's master plan is not the population of the earth, but rather the achievement of "the full number of the elect."

This explains why it is so fundamentally important for mother and father to nourish a genuine and profound love for each other, and at the same time to develop great courage, a noble spirit of sacrifice, and deep love for their children.

14

IS UGLINESS OR BEAUTY MORE DANGEROUS?

In a recent discussion, we got into an argument on the question of whether, in the moral order, it is ugliness or beauty that is the more dangerous. Could you help us find an answer?

Beauty is a perfection. What is perfect and better in itself cannot, of itself, be dangerous, or more dangerous than the lack of proper perfection and harmony.

In this respect, allow me to tell a simple and moving story that I saw enacted on a train one day: a German girl was behaving very badly towards a colored soldier;

at a certain point in the conversation a lady who was particularly upset with the girl's behavior turned to her and said: "If you were not so ugly yourself, maybe you wouldn't give in so easily to the temptation to be so nasty." Ugliness is a danger in many respects; inferiority complexes frequently manifest themselves in an effort to call attention to oneself at any cost.

But to answer the question more basically, we must first of all determine precisely what we mean by ugliness and beauty. A human person is beautiful when we can tell, by looking at him, that he has been created in the "image and likeness of God" and that this likeness shines out in his conduct, in what he does and says, and, above all, in his face. The old grandmother, her aged face covered with wrinkles, bowed under the weight of years, can be very beautiful: everything about her is a mark of goodness, maturity, composure. A man is beautiful when his body, for example, is not just a perfect model of muscle and development, but also a model of strength of mind and body and spirit firmly guided by free will. A girl is beautiful when the expression on her face and the form and posture of her body are a revelation of spirit, goodness, inner purity.

Beautiful or Ugly?

Even a "beauty queen" can be ugly from the authentically human point of view, that is, when her expression and attitude give evidence of stupidity, materialism, foolishness, and self-centeredness. From a purely animal point of view, it is always possible to ask a panel of judges whether a certain person, who happens to be characterized primarily by a strong element of sex appeal, together with a well-developed and exciting body, can be called beautiful or not. But from the point of view of authentic human beauty, it is impossible not to feel some compassion for such ugliness and rupugnant lack of harmony. How can we call a person beautiful if the lower elements not only veil but even negate the higher elements of beauty which must exist within her?

Modern advertizing has succeeded in spreading a false concept of beauty. It teaches us to admire, as an ideal of human beauty, creamy smooth skin, or a skin that has been bronzed on the beach, the Beatle style hair cut, etc. The Christian's duty is to correct this and similar false concepts of beauty, by his example and by his conversation, and to spread an appreciation of the true ideals.

Particularly, we must reflect more seriously on the true Christian criterion of beauty when we are faced with the problem of decent and proper dress. In this area we must consider beauty as anything that manifests the human person's intention to be beautiful in the eyes of God and in the eyes of persons who have faith; everything that shows that such a person is cultivating his body and his soul as one harmonious and indivisible whole, cultivating it in such a way as to call attention to the promise of God's own beauty.

There might well be occasions which a woman or a girl will need to pay particular attention to her appearance, in order not to lead others into temptation by the neglect of her dress and grooming, especially men who are afflicted with an inferiority complex. But more frequently, much more frequently in fact, they will do well to avoid excessive and overly refined attention to externals like dress and cosmetics and jewelry in order not to hide the true beauty that is within.

What is better, beauty or ugliness?

Every person must accept himself as he is and try, within the limits of his own potential and the requirements of the world he lives in, to cultivate, first a high degree of beauty of soul, and, in union with this, intelligently, the harmony and beauty of his body as well.

15

DOES THE CHURCH PERMIT PAINLESS CHILDBIRTH?

I would like to know whether or not the Church permits painless childbirth, and since there are so many different kinds today, which ones are permissible and which ones are not.

After the Fall of our first parents, God pronounced this sentence on woman: "I will greatly multiply your pain in childbearing; in pain you shall bring forth children, yet your desire shall be for your husband, and he shall rule over you" (Gen. 3, 16). On the basis of this text, many people have drawn the conclusion that a woman is not allowed to take any measures to alleviate her

sufferings in childbirth, and that the man has the right
to be lord over her. Such a conclusion, however, is
quite false.

The biblical text does not give either a command or
a prohibition in this respect; it merely indicates that,
as a result of original sin, these pains will always be the
woman's lot. Just as the man is not bound to sow the
seed in the ground and simply allow the earth to produce
thorns and thistles, even so the woman is not obliged
to passively undergo the pains of childbirth. She is
redeemed just like man, and this means that she no
longer needs to look upon pain as a curse, that she is
free to accept it as a blessing, and a sharing in the cross
of Christ.

Childbirth, with all its pains and suffering, is, for
the woman — as St. Paul expressly states in his Letter to
Timothy (I Tim. 2, 15) — a source of blessing and a way
of salvation. She is free to combat, and seek to avoid,
with a peaceful conscience and by the use of licit means,
all the pain that might otherwise diminish her joy as
a mother. Pius XII made this very clear statement in an
allocution delivered in 1956.

Conscious Motherhood

The Church is pleased to note the fact that the position of woman, in our modern society, is considerably
improved, and that man recognizes her as equal in human
dignity to himself. In like manner, the Church is happy
whenever medicine discovers anything to alleviate or
eliminate the pains of childbirth. The birth of a child,

like the experience of death, is one of the fundamental moments in human existence. It is truly a wonderful thing to behold a Christian going to meet death as he would a friend, fully conscious and facing it in union with the death of Christ, buoyed up by the sure hope of resurrection. In the same way, a mother should face the moment of childbirth without using any medical assistance that could make her lose consciousness, at least as far as possible, simply in order to taste the joy of this wonderful event.

Thus, in terms of principle, we must express a preference for those methods of painless childbirth which do not involve the loss, at least the complete loss, of consciousness. Modern applied psychology has evolved some methods that considerably if not completely eliminate the pains of childbirth without involving any danger for the mother of the child, and without depriving the mother of the joy of this blessed moment.

For the rest, it is obvious that no conscientious doctor would recommend or prescribe anything that would endanger the child's birth.

Finally, the therapeutic elimination or alleviation of the pains of childbirth can be justified on the basis of a simple historical consideration. In former times, for many women, the pains of childbirth were not so severe as they are today in our overcivilized urban culture. For many women, the pains of childbirth are psychologically aggravated by the fact that they do not experience the joy they should feel at the blossoming of new life within them. A healthy sense of joy at the prospect of having a baby, on the part of the mother and on the part of the civilization in which she lives, would already be enough in itself to alleviate much of this misgiving. Where this joy is not to be found, or not sufficiently developed, every form of medical or psychological intervention is a real blessing.

16

NUMBER OF CHILDREN

My wife and I have had two children now, a girl of six and a boy of three; prior to their birth there was a pregnancy which did not come to term. During the last pregnancy, at the beginning of the third month, my wife suffered an attack of phlebitis which had to be treated first in the hospital and then at home. As a result, her right leg has remained a little larger than her left leg for want of proper circulation. Thanks be to God we both work so we are not in any great economic difficulty. But we would both also like to be assured that we have really done our proper Christian duty. That is why I am writing to you. Our boy is three years old now and we are concerned about acting according to the teachings of the Church. The question is: should we have another child? As far as our economic condition is concerned, we would be inclined to answer yes. With respect to the possible complications to my wife's health, we do not know what to say. I, in particular, am afraid; but I do not want this to prevent our doing the will of God. Is it proper for my wife to risk dangers that are more serious than what she faced during her last pregnancy? In an effort to resolve my doubts, I now ask whether this line of conduct is morally right: we plan to have no other children (for the sake of my wife's health) and instead of having another child, we will give economic help (as long as it is possible, in at least a limited way, until one of us has to stop working) to two children of some needy friends. During the meantime we will practice rhythm and make use of the other new moral methods suggested by the Church. Is this all right? Or is it just a rationalization on our part? Is it, maybe, only a subtle way of avoiding the responsibility that the Church would seem to leave to the conscience of married people?

Many thanks for your letter. Your way of thinking and your sincere effort to discover the will of God are exactly what we mean when we speak of responsible parenthood. First of all, you are sincerely trying to learn and fulfill the will of God; this is not an easy thing to do, because frequently what appears to be "responsibility" is actually only selfishness and looking for our own advantage. Secondly, even in the business of forming your own consience, you are willing to be guided by the experience and direction of the Church. Thirdly, you show real love for your own children and a genuine appreciation of children, no matter whose they are. Thus you would like to have more children if the health of your wife permitted, and since you cannot, you desire to help other people's children. Finally, by undertaking the tangible support of the poor, you are trying to guard against the danger of being guided by selfish interests and a lazy unwillingness to make such important decisions for yourself.

Birth Control

You have understood, and understood very well, that the responsible parenthood of practicing Catholics is many miles removed from the selfish practice of birth control, even in the choice of methods. It is obvious to you that a Catholic husband and wife must always nurture a great respect for conjugal union, even when there are just and even binding reasons for not wanting to risk another pregnancy at the time. The things that vitiate the integrity of conjugal union as the authentic "knowing of each other" spoken of in the Bible are not even taken into account by them, since they live in the constant presence of God. And thus, even when, during such periods, they are concerned with maintaining the tenderness and devotion of their mutual love, it is obvious that they cannot even think of resorting to methods which could even be an affront to their human dignity.

The Church — especially Pius XII and his successors — approves the practice of periodic continence in this and similar cases. This corresponds to the pastoral advice given by St. Paul to the Corinthians: "Do not refuse one another except perhaps by agreement for a season, that you may devote yourselves to prayer; but then come together again, lest Satan tempt you through lack of self-control" (I Cor. 7, 5).

Periodic Continence

Periodic continence, in such a case, does not represent an effort to avoid responsibility; rather it is an expression of real responsibility with respect to the health of the mother and with respect to the children who have already been born, just as it is also a responsible attitude towards the act of conjugal union which is carried out in all its integrity. Periodic continence is good not only because it imposes a sacrifice, but primarily because it is an expression of respect and fidelity to the order established by God in the exercise and manifestation of conjugal love. The Church has condemned other methods of regulating the frequency of birth, not because they succeed in regulating conception in cases of genuine and justified need, but simply because they violate the integrity and dignity of conjugal union.

As a result, we are allowed to make full use of the modern discoveries of science, like plotting a temperature chart, in order to make the practice of rhythm as effective as possible. Still everyone knows that this method does involve a certain margin of risk, greater or lesser according to individual cases. In same cases even — in cases much more serious even than your own, where the mother's life is clearly at stake — it simply cannot be applied because the woman's menstrual cycle is too irregular. In very many of these cases — and your case might well be one of them too — it is morally licit, on the one hand, to want to put off or even exclude the possibility of a new pregnancy, and on the other hand it would be just as correct to run the risk of a new pregnancy and trust in God: life without risk of any kind is not a healthy normal life. Your letter speaks of "new moral methods suggested by the Church." As a priest and a student of moral theology, I cannot help saying that I am happy to note that you will not consider just any method, until its moral licitness has been definitely established by the Church. But I must also inform you that the mere discussion of these matters among competent people (viz. regarding other methods their moral licitness or sinfulness, the risk they involve or do not involve for the health of the woman, etc.) cannot as yet be said to constitute an adequate rule or confidence for the faithful. This is even more true in our case, from the moment that Paul VI has expressly warned us not to anticipate his judgment. The serious study that these problems are receiving at the hands of the supreme authorities of our Church is a further reason for us to give them full obedience.

17

THE CASE OF THE WOMAN WHO CANNOT HAVE CHILDREN WITHOUT SERIOUS RISK

I am willing to admit that, in having children, we should not be exclusively preoccupied with economic restrictions, and have more trust in Divine Providence. But as to your statement that it is still morally licit to have children even when the life of the mother is in danger, this I find it hard to agree with. How can a good Catholic believe in risking other people's lives? In my opinion, a man who is about to marry should first make sure that his future wife will not run any risk to her health in becoming pregnant, and, to make sure, he should insist on regular visits to the doctor, and provide the proper medical care. If the doctor says that having a baby would cost the mother's life, then the man must either refuse to marry her, or be content to love her only spiritually. But if the danger is discovered only after their marriage, then, in my opinion, the man has a strict obligation to observe continence (not periodic continence which always involves a certain element of risk, but absolute and uninterrupted continence). Otherwise he is nothing more or less than a murderer, since he is guilty of a homicidal attempt

upon human life, and is violating the fifth com-
mandment which forbids us to make deliberate
attempts upon our own life or that of other
people. Finally I think that if his own sex in-
stincts are too strong for him to resist them, and
husband and wife have sex relations in such a
way as to deliberately avoid offspring, then I
think that the sin they commit is still less serious
than the sin of murder.

This letter is interesting for many reasons, and for the many excellent ideas which it contains. Thus, for example, I can only agree with the writer when he says that a husband does not have the right to expose his wife, on the basis of a unilateral decision, to a serious danger to her life, particularly when his only real motive is the satisfaction of his lower instincts.

Responsible parenthood always means that both parents have to examine the problem, in their own conscience, in the sight of God, and reach a common decision. Especially when there is a question of running a serious risk to health or life on the wife's part, the decision has to be the result of common effort.

When there is some probability that a new pregnancy will seriously threaten the wife's life, then the fifth commandment, their mutual love, normal respect for life and the care of the children already born would all suggest putting off the prospect of increasing the family. In such a case, for example, it is better to consider the possibility of adopting an orphan.

Most of the time, however, it is, today, merely a

question of running a more or less serious risk to the wife's state of health, since modern medicine is almost always in a position to save the life of the mother and the baby.

On the other hand, the parents always have the right to run such a risk, just as they have the right to take up mountain climbing or train as astronauts. And when we are speaking of truly Christian parents, the really important thing for them is that they realize their decision is not ever guided simply by the satisfaction of a physical instinct.

Something Great and Holy

Allow me, however, to make one or the other observation on this expression: "satisfaction of a lower instinct." The Manicheans, the Gnostics, and, in their turn, the Albigensians, as well as other sects, all looked down upon human sexuality as something base and vulgar. The Church, however, maintains the greatest respect for human sexuality, as something created by God, and it is precisely this attitude of respect that explains why she condemns every abuse in this area as the most serious sin.

Human sexuality is something marvelously noble because it is destined to further and nurture the spark of human life within the bosom of human marriage. The conjugal act is a cooperation in the creative love of God. And even during those periods and circumstances in which it cannot possibly give rise to a new life, it still remains something great, something holy, sanctified by the sacrament of matrimony, created as an expression of the profound, tender, and lasting love of the marriage partners. This is the act by which they prove their mutual devotion, promised in the sacrament itself, and revive the mutual love that leads them to desire children, to make them share in their own affection. It is the sex act that safeguards their mutual fidelity and promotes the harmony that is a necessary prerequisite for the proper upbringing of their children.

Sexuality is profaned and degraded when it is abused in the interests of simple self-satisfaction. This self-centered "pleasure" does not make people happy. Sexuality in marriage is the source of joy for body and spirit precisely in the measure in which husband and wife attempt to satisfy each other and make each other a gift of their own love. When they seek only their own individual sexual satisfaction, they degrade themselves and they eventually end up feeling sick and disgusted with each other.

Act of Self-Recognition

Human sexuality is completely different from animal sexuality. The animal is guided by instinct and he copulates when fecundation and generation are possible. Human sexuality is subject to human reason and the love that comes from God. As a human phenomenon, it is related to the phenomenon of language. In language, man expresses himself. The conjugal act is like a mutual "self-recognition." It is the full expression of the nobility, altruism, and attention and love that husband and wife feel towards each other.

The act of masturbation, when it is deliberately and freely willed, is not only a sin against sex, but it is also an expression of all the self-centeredness, isolationism, loneliness, and self-seeking that is possible in a man. Sexual satisfaction with a person of the opposite sex, enjoyed by two persons who are not married to each other, or adultery, is simply a lie told by the entire body. What was destined, in the plans of the Creator and in the force of nature, to be the expression of absolute fidelity is here made to express the precise opposite. The reason that these acts are so perverse is simply this: human sexuality is not something vulgar or common, not some "base instinct," but a masterpiece of God's creation.

The virtue of chastity does not consist in being immune to every sexual attraction and instinct, but in the profound respect for everything connected with the mystery of sex, for marriage and for virginity alike, and also in the reasoned control of the sex instinct and its reasoned, respectful and loving use in marriage.

18

WHAT ABOUT THIS "CATHOLIC" PILL THAT
IS SUPPOSED TO TAKE CARE OF BIRTH CON-
TROL?

The Church is strongly opposed to a movement, very
much in vogue today, which sees the child as an obstacle
to the happiness of marriage or which tends towards
childlessness on grounds of simple selfishness. On the
other hand, as I have abundantly proved by documents
in my book, *Marriage in the Modern World,* the Church
proposes the principle of responsible parenthood.

This principle means that the parents must desire
to have as many children as they can, not simply bring
into the world, but also care for and bring up properly,
taking into account the individual gifts and potential
with which God has blessed them. Translated into
prayer, this means: "How can we give thanks to God
for all the blessings he has given us?" It is an obligation
that is serious, and it demands serious reflection in the
parents common purpose, and great prayer, in order to
recognize the will of God and live up to it with real
courage.

According to the different cases, responsible parenthood can imply the joyous acceptance of the twelfth
child, or, most of the time, a reasonable spacing between
children, or sometimes even the sorrowful realization
that it is impossible to have more children.

Means for Achieving Responsible Parenthood

What are the means that husband and wife have at their disposal in carrying out these principles?

The Church has repeatedly and energetically condemned every method of birth control that goes counter to the dignity and natural fulness of the conjugal union. When attention is fixed solely on the excitation and satisfaction of the sex instinct, marriage relations simply degenerate, little by little, into a distasteful system of reciprocal sexual satisfaction.

On the other hand, a lengthy and complete abstinence from intimate marriage relations is beyond the strength of husband and wife, as St. Paul already recognizes (1 Cor. 7, 5). In this respect, when we presume too much upon our own strength, or that of the marriage partner — apart from the case of a special gift or calling by God himself — we are simply endangering the whole framework of our marriage. One possible method has been repeatedly indicated by the Church, the use of periodic continence. It is a disposition of Divine Providence that God has made woman fertile only during a few days of her menstrual cycle, and infertile all the other time. Man is not acting arbitrarily when he makes use of this knowledge he has acquired of the laws of nature, after examining his conscience in the sight of God, humbly and faithfully, and deciding, together with his wife, that for the time being they cannot responsibly give birth to another child. The big problem, however, lies in the fact that many couples are not sufficiently well instructed in the science of accurately

computing which are the fertile days and which are the
infertile ones, whereas in other cases it is a natural irreg-
ularity in the menstrual cycle that makes it impossible
to calculate these days with anything approaching the
necessary precision. The problem is even more difficult
for men who have to work at some distance away from
home and can thus spend only a few days at a time with
their wives.

What is to be done when, on the one hand, there are
serious and reasonable motives for not wanting to increase the number of children in the family, while, on
the other hand, it is equally impossible to make use of
the infertile periods?

Is there Really a "Catholic" Pill?

For some time now there has been a lot of discussion
all over the world about the so-called "Catholic" pill.
Has it really been discovered, and what is it?

A certain number of moralists, in the USA and in
England, seem to have put their hopes in a pill offered
for sale some two years ago, and not yet completely
tested or guaranteed, as a solution to the many difficulties
that married people encounter in the course of their
married life. The pill is called "duphaston" and is supposed to be able to completely normalize the menstrual
cycle during the entire time that the woman takes it.
The woman — and this is an essential point — does
nothing to change her normal functions. Ovulation
occurs, infallibly, at the proper moment. The new pill,
like its predecessors which have been popular for some

eight years now (Enovid, Norlutin, Anovlar, etc.), is an artificial progesterone, but with a somewhat different molecular composition and containing other chemical ingredients.

The preceding pills are those which Pope Pius XII took into consideration in his statements of September 12, 1958, which was negative in tone, and which immediately became the subject of a lively discussion even though many authorities declared for the opposition since the effect of such pills was the temporary impairment of ovulation, excluding it with sufficient certainty to preclude the possibility of conception. The discussion turned primarily about the licitness of taking the pills during the period of lactation.

The question asked today is this: is "duphaston," the new pill, more "Catholic" than the old one, that is, less open to criticism for a really well formed conscience?

For the time being, the answer must be no. In fact there are some conscientious gynecologists (who are well known) who have expressed some fears that the new pill will permanently impair or inhibit the healthy and normal development of an ovum that is eventually fertilized. Thus, until this problem has been completely cleared up, it is impossible for moralists to advise the use of the pill.

There are, however, those who hope to be able to perfect this new discovery, to eliminate all the dangers, and then to put it up for sale, with full advertizing and publicity, as the "Catholic" pill.

Whatever the case may be, even in the face of such an eventuality, the Catholic moralist feels an obligation

to make a few remarks, without claiming to give anything like a definitive judgment.

Obviously, from the point of view of biological function, there is a difference between the old pill and the
new one, and the same thing can be said from the point
of view of moral obligation; as a matter of fact, the new
pill would still require the practice of periodic continence, for about four days a month.

Moral Obligation

Still — and this is the whole point — the fact that we
must speak of a "Catholic" pill, together with the background behind this expression, makes us appear somewhat ridiculous in the eyes of non-Catholics. Is the
difference between the two pills really as great as the
difference between heaven (no sin at all) and hell
(mortal sin)? Fundamentally, and as a matter of principle, is there anything more natural about effecting a
total pause in the female organism by using the older
pill, which impedes ovulation but augments the woman's
fertility for the future (when she stops taking the pill),
than there is in definitively fixing and regulating the
ovulation cycle by means of an intervention, equally
artificial, in the natural functions of the body? (In this
question, ultimately, of course, it is the gynecologists who
have the greater competence to make a decision.) Is it
wise to place such great hopes in the discovery of a pill
for the eternal salvation of husband and wife?

The decisive element is and remains the constant
moral effort, loyal and humble, to arrive at a genuine

love. If we do everything in our power, if we pray steadfastly for the grace and strength to fulfill better and more fully whatever we have not succeeded in doing yet, if we sincerely repent of our weakness and our offenses, we are on the way to being saved, with or without a pill. This does not mean, naturally, that we are not to make every effort to investigate the laws of nature, in an effort to help all men of good will. It means only that we must not expect to find the solution in an overly nice and hair-splitting series of distinctions.

It is particularly discouraging to note that some Catholic circles have expressed a decidedly negative attitude on this question, while others have fully accepted the new discovery. In this manner, on the one hand, they lose sight of the understanding and sympathy that is owing to those married couples who find themselves in a difficult situation but are still, timidly and cautiously, making their way towards a conjugal love that is more and more perfect. And on the other hand, they tend to forget the fact that, in the last analysis, married happiness and eternal salvation both demand a decided effort towards holiness, and a willingness to face the necessary renunciations that life imposes. The vision of the whole complex of this question is always much more important than any individual casuistic solution.

19

CELIBACY BY FORCE AND CELIBACY FOR LOVE OF THE KINGDOM OF HEAVEN

The Catholic Church of Rome does not admit the possibility of divorce, or a separation in which the innocent partner, who is not responsible for the break and the failure of the marriage, is free to contract another marriage. What I want to know is what value is there in a forced celibacy, one that is imposed by authority? The Oriental rites, so I am told, have a much more reasonable attitude towards this problem.

The activity of the Egyptian Archbishop Zoghbi in the recent Council, calling attention to the practices of the Oriental Churches, which allow the innocent partner freedom to remarry, has reintroduced the question of divorce and separation. The doctrine and discipline of the Roman Church in this matter is too well known, and too rigorously faithful to the Gospel, to need any words of explanation. But there is a further element that does need discussion — as the letter suggests — what about the value of a celibacy that is forced upon a person?

Not All Can Grasp

One day when Jesus had explained to the disciples that the Mosaic Law, which allowed a man to put away his wife and remarry, was no longer valid in the Messianic Era, in the fulness of redemption, they still did not understand, and said "If this is the case of a man with respect to his wife, it is not a good idea to marry" (Matt. 19, 10). Jesus took advantage of their imperfect understanding, and their reaction to his statement, to proclaim the great mystery of "celibacy for love of the Kingdom of heaven." But first he recalls the supernatural atmosphere that surrounds the married state and the indissoluble fidelity required of the marriage partners. "Not all men can grasp this word, but only those to whom it has been granted" (Matt. 19, 11). Man, as he is and as he acts since the time of Adam, is not in a position to grasp the doctrine of absolute fidelity, which is valid even when the other marriage partner has acted unjustly and is at fault. Now the word of Christ should be enough to convince every son of Adam, because it is absolutely worthy of faith. But a purely intellectual understanding and acceptance of Christ's word, based on the value of our Savior's testimony, is still very far removed from a practical and existential understanding, especially when the situation becomes serious and strikes close to home and imposes the renunciation of a new marriage.

When Christ says that only those to whom it has been granted are able to grasp his word, we must never doubt that he will grant this grace to anyone who wants to be his disciple. All such men are really called to holiness. But first we need to take a decisive stand in following him, so that we can understand the meaning behind the indissolubility of marriage even in the most difficult conditions, and hold to it as a principle with real conviction.

Total and Irrevocable Assent

Those who have the courage to give their total and irrevocable assent to the marriage bond and to remain faithful even at the price of great sacrifice can count on the solemn promise made by Christ, a promise not unlike the promise that he made in the same context as to those who refrain from marriage for the love of the kingdom of heaven. Christian marriage is much closer to the mystery of "celibacy for the love of the kingdom of heaven" than to that conception of married life which had grown up among the descendants of Adam by reason of the hardness of their heart.

Christ clearly distinguishes the various meanings that celibacy can have for a man: "There are eunuchs who have been so from birth, and there are eunuchs who have been made eunuchs by men, and there are eunuchs who are made themselves eunuchs for the sake of the kingdom of heaven. He who is able to receive this, let him receive it" (Matt. 19, 12).

There are many ways of depriving a person of the possibility of marrying. Sometimes it is the tyrannical will of the parents who want the son or daughter all for themselves, or who try to induce them to contract a marriage that is condemned to failure from the outset, or simply not desired by the interested parties. In centuries past it was, sometimes, difficult economic conditions which prevented many young people from having

a family of their own. Thus, considered from a purely
human point of view, we can only sympathize with the
sad lot of the separated husband and wife whose condition is the result of their own fault, or the fault of
one of them. Those who are abandoned by their legitimate wife or husband, through no fault of their own,
and forced to live a long life of celibacy do deserve our
sympathy and our consideration.

In this respect many people wonder whether this
does not perhaps represent a real curse even for a
Christian, that is, even for one who knows that he is
redeemed and a friend of Christ.

It is true that this situation is the bitter fruit of sin.
It is terribly unjust to deprive anyone of the cherished
joys of marriage, and this is a consideration that should
be kept well in mind by those young men who court a
young lady for several years, putting her off with a
promise of marriage, and then abandoning her without
good reason. But the man who faithfully loves God and
orients his life in terms of the light of grace, cannot,
basically, regard this as a curse. "For those who love
God everything works out for the good" (Rom. 8, 28).
The man who embraces the cross of Christ will also
have a share in the resurrection.

What initially had only the bitter taste of a celibacy
imposed by force of circumstances or the injustice of
man, becomes, for the man of faith, and always with
the help of God's grace, something completely new and
full of meaning, a "celibacy for the love of the kingdom
of God." At first he will likely have no further choice
than to accept his personal loss and misery with his

inner eye fixed upon the kingdom of a crucified and risen
Christ. But along his private way of the cross he will
soon come to understand that it is good to live that way
since God has permitted it and helped him to "understand." This is a somewhat different path than that
of joyously learning to understand the meaning of virginity in the springtime of life. It is a path that is beset
with great depths of suffering, frequently very sharp
and bitter. But the man who commits himself to our
Savior's care will one day experience the blessed discovery that is expressed in these words: "O blessed loss,
which has brought me so close to God!"

If some Eastern Churches allow an unjustly abandoned husband and wife to remarry, this is not a sign that
they approve of such a step. It is only an evidence of
mercy and kindness. In earlier times, the whole community of the faithful would cooperate to help the
innocent victim, exhorting him to transform the celibacy
thus forced upon him into a supernaturally fruitful form
of life, out of love for the kingdom of heaven. We can
well understand the sentiments of mercy which have led
some of the Eastern Churches to refrain from excom-
municating from their sacramental communion those
who, notwithstanding all the spiritual support and aid
the Church has to offer, were not in a position to understand their enforced celibacy, and turn it into a thing
of great interior beauty, but have yielded to the temptation of remarrying. But we must also bear in mind
the fact that these Churches have never given unqual-
ified approval to this course of action.

As the same Archbishop Zoghbi stressed in a second

interview, this practice does not imply a denial of the indissolubility of marriage; it merely represents a very restricted possibility within Church discipline, applicable only in the case of those who are unjustly abandoned or repudiated through no fault of their own. This dispensation is considered as an act of mercy and a considerate method of accepting the lesser of two evils. But it can never be conceded to the partner who has actually abandoned the other or, by his own fault, provoked the other to leave. "The wife should not separate from her husband (but if she does, let her remain single or else be reconciled with her husband) — and the husband should not divorce his wife" (I Cor. 7, 10-11). For the rest, as the Patriarch Maximus has pointed out, the Eastern Churches themselves are not agreed in establishing whether or not such exceptional practices and such mild discipline in the case of the abandoned husband or wife are in conformity with Sacred Scripture.

The Church is Faithful to the Gospel

In the same way, we who live according to the practice of the Roman Catholic Church, rigorously faithful to the Gospel which forbids the separated husband or wife to remarry, even when it is a question of unjust abandonment, must be equally understanding and merciful towards those who have failed in this respect. Our kindness, our understanding, and our friendship can, in many cases, prove to be the factor that helps them to rediscover the way of salvation. Such a person, after remarrying while his former marriage partner is still alive, if he repents of the step he has taken and does everything he can to undo the evil he has done, if he perseveringly prays for the grace to do what he knows he should but cannot yet bring himself to do, then, in his heart and in his intentions, such a person is already on the right path and can confidently trust in the mercy of God. Greater kindness and more generous and ready understanding on the part of his friends and family might, in many cases, have kept him from deciding to remarry in the first place.

The true solution, in perfect keeping with the message of the Gospel, is this: it is absolutely necessary for the Church community and those who are close to a person upon whom the circumstances of his life have forced the practice of celibacy to help him recognize and "understand" the religious meaning of his condition; they need, especially, great kindness, real genuine friendship, and close intimacy insofar as it is possible. In addition to this, there is much help to be found in a satisfying professional activity, active participation in the life of the Church, and all the thousand little joys that anyone can find for himself in his everyday living. An essential element is always prayer and the spirit of sacrifice, together with cooperation with God's grace. In cases such as these, a particularly important role is to be played by those persons, of deep personal faith, who know how to say a few words that are illuminating and filled with faith, to help reveal the meaning of this new situation of life, until the party concerned can himself arrive at a position in which he will see everything in the light of God's kingdom.

20

WHY IS THERE NOT SOME PREPARATION FOR CELIBACY TOO?

With respect to the sad case of souls consecrated to God who are lost, I have been considering some means to diminish, if not eliminate, the great number of defections. Noting that a very large percentage of these defections occur between the years 25 to 35 (if I am not mistaken), why could there not be, for example, a sort of "novitiate" between the diaconate and the priesthood, lasting for ten years or so? Meantime the deacon would be free to engage in all kinds of pastoral activity, acting as assistant to the parish priest and working in every field of the apostolate, even working with women, excepting, obviously, hearing confessions and saying Mass. After ten years of such activity he would be required to make a final decision.

Fidelity to the marriage bond "until death do us part" and fidelity to the vow of chastity and the obligation of celibacy, freely assumed, "for love of the kingdom of heaven," must be maintained side by side. Each must be a constant praise of Christ, *the* Faithful Man par excellence. That is precisely why preparation for marriage and preparation for celibacy are each so very important.

In many countries, engaged people have to undergo a lengthy catechumenate, composed of prayer and instruction, with a view towards acquiring a full awareness of what the vow of fidelity, taken at the altar, really means for them and for the whole Church. The Church is even more careful in the preparation of her future priests, in order to make them truly fit for the practice of their ministry, and especially to guarantee that they will give evidence of holiness in a life that is freely chaste and celibate.

And since the difficulties in this respect have vastly multiplied today, it is no wonder that the Church takes more and greater pains to make the vital evidence of this undivided love and fidelity to Christ even more splendid and trust-worthy.

Perhaps in the future she will change her attitude towards those who have proved themselves less faithful to their obligations and give no hope of improvement. In individual cases she might handle such problems differently than she has in recent decades. But this does not mean a relaxation or, even less, an abandonment of the ideal of celibacy. On the contrary, all her efforts are aimed precisely at strengthening and reinvigorating it and making it a more worthy and fitting testimony of fidelity to this calling. It is precisely for this reason that, in a given case, it might be a wise solution not only to remove an unfaithful priest from his priestly ministry and functions, but also to absolve him of his vow of celibacy, to reduce him to the state of penitent and, mercifully, to allow him to marry after having deprived him of all his priestly obligations. Still, even in such cases — making an exception for those individuals who are pathologically predisposed — the parties in question should be made to feel the great evil and injustice they have committed in violating the fidelity they have freely sworn to keep, and to understand why they have to be treated as penitents.

The same thing is true in the case of a religious, a monk or a brother, who, after having taken his solemn and perpetual vows, requests to be released and wants to marry. The Church allows them to go their way in peace, but she seriously admonishes them to do penance for the grave act of infidelity they have committed.

Religious Novitiate

In order to reduce the number of such problems in the case of religious vows, the Church has, in our day, insisted that perpetual profession be preceded, not only by the regular novitiate, but also by a period of trial, which can vary in length from three to six years, during which only temporary vows are taken. This temporary profession is made with the firm intention of later making a perpetual profession. If, however, during the years which follow, the person in question comes to realize that he cannot live up to this lofty ideal, he is free to leave the monastery, or he may be invited to do so by the superior.

For my part, I do not see why the Catholic Church of the Latin rite cannot adopt the same discipline in the case of priestly celibacy. In the near future, in some regions, we shall most probably see the diaconate con-

ferred on married men, religiously mature and eager to
be of service, without any obligation to observe celibacy.
But the majority of the bishops at the Council still
expressed the opinion that, in the case of young men
who are not yet married, the diaconate should be con-
ferred only with the corresponding obligation of celibacy.

Praises of Celibacy

In my humble opinion, it does not seem impossible
that this obligation should be interpreted — in the not
too distant future — in a somewhat similar manner as the
temporary vows of religious. There would, thus, be a
true obligation, but it would not exclude the possibility
of returning to the lay state, whenever, after a certain
period of time, it was obvious that the person in question
was unequal to the obligation. Only those whose conduct was in harmony with their vow, like religious
during the years of their temporary profession, should
then be ordained priests at the end of their service as
deacons. Together with their ordination, the obligation
of celibacy would become a perpetual one, just as it is
in the case of perpetual profession. This, as I have
already mentioned, is only my own opinion. Perhaps
the Church authorities will see fit to inaugurate something similar to this, or something even better, in an
effort to reduce the distressing number of scandals involving priestly infidelity. At all events, one thing is,
and ought to be, clear to everyone: every Christian
should have a deep respect for celibacy, pray for his
priests, and avoid everything that might lead them into

temptation. Priestly infidelity is a wound to the Mystical Body of Christ. Those unfortunate men who have violated their fidelity do deserve our understanding. But on the other hand, the words of our Savior are still true: "Woe to those who give scandal!" Many catastrophes could be avoided if every Catholic girl understood the grandeur of celibacy. The love of the priest belongs indivisibly to God and the immortal souls for whom he works. No one must dare to monopolize it exclusively for oneself. The celibate reminds the world, in words of fire, of the stern admonition of Scripture: "Holy to the Lord."

21

CAN SPIES DELIBERATELY TAKE THEIR OWN LIVES?

I recently read an American book on counter-espionage in various countries. One section was explaining the proper conduct for an espionage agent who has been captured by the enemy. The agent, in substance, is supposed to take his own life (by taking special pills which contain poison), rather than risk revealing the State secrets he knows to the enemy. Now I would like to ask you: what does religion have to say about this advice? Doesn't our Savior say that no one has a right to take his own life?

The commandment of God, "Thou shalt not kill," absolutely forbids any unauthorized attempt, fully deliberate and perpetrated in full possession of the senses, against one's own life or the life of another person. Only God is the master of life and death. Still, his commandment needs to be properly understood. When the State, in an effort to defend innocent life, condemns murderers and serious criminals to death, it is not transgressing the fifth commandment, because it is not acting irresponsibly and without authority. The same is to be said with respect to the legitimate defense of one's own life: when a person cannot defend his own life or his neighbor's life without killing the unjust aggressor, this is not murder. In all these cases, it is, ultimately, the condemned man who is responsible for his own death.

In war — excepting, of course, for unjust wars — it is morally right either to sacrifice one's own life or to kill the soldiers on the enemy side. The man who sacrifices his life to defend his country when it is unjustly attacked, or to defend his own existence, is not a suicide. By offering himself in such a sacrifice, he is not arbitrarily disposing of his own life, fully and deliberately, but rather fulfilling an obligation of justice or love. The pilot who, in time of war, upon orders from his superiors, crashes his plane into the enemy fleet is not considered a suicide but a hero — always presupposing, of course, that it is a just war, fought in defense of his country, and this is a condition that is not always fulfilled, as history clearly shows.

These examples cast some light on and help us to judge the case of the spy, as mentioned in the letter.

It is not an easy case, and moralists do not always give the same answers. When a man first enlists in the espionage service, the first point to be considered is whether or not he is working in the service of a just cause. In such a case his work might serve to circumvent a terrible war, if he can, for example, succeed in unmasking the secret plans of an unjust regime. The spy who undertakes such a position, working for his country, must realize that, in certain circumstances, he might well be called upon to sacrifice his life.

Not Suicide

Thus, in my opinion, suicide does not enter into the problem of the spy who takes his own life "in obedience to orders received," when, in a given circumstance, he is morally certain that he cannot perform his service in behalf of his country and world peace without resorting to this extreme solution.

Still, the opinions of leading moralists are not in harmony on this subject, and the proposed solution cannot be considered as definitive.

In order to better explain the precise bearing of the answer, and the reasoning that leads to it, let us consider the following elements:

1. The spy, in this case, is not acting freely and deliberately in taking his own life, but is under orders.

2. The spy is not acting out of selfish interests, because he is free to choose this solution only when it is the only way to safeguard a secret of state or make a decisive

and significant contribution to the cause of world peace or the defense of his country.

3. We must take into account the ruthlessness of modern dictators who have ways, not only of torturing him, but also making him "sing" the way they want.

4. We must also presuppose that the spy has undertaken this work, not for personal gain or any other unworthy motives, but only because he is convinced that he will be making a useful and even significant contribution to world peace.

5. When, finally, the opposing power is controlled by a just and human system of government which treats spies justly and humanely, then he no longer has a sufficient and just reason to take his own life or, to put it in other words, to sacrifice his own life, in obedience to the orders received.

In fact, whenever it is not a question of an absolutely necessary sacrifice in behalf of a just cause, then the death in question would be an act of full personal responsibility and mature deliberation against one's own life, and this, of course, cannot ever be allowed.

Finally, we must recall that if the person involved is convinced, in conscience, that the order he has received to take his own life in case of arrest is not a just order, he is not morally free to take up espionage work, to begin with.

22

IS IT MORALLY RIGHT TO WILL YOUR BODY TO MEDICAL RESEARCH?

I am a blood donor and some years ago I also signed a statement willing the corneas of my eyes for the use of the blind after my death. I would like to write in my will that if there are other organs in my body that are useful for humanity, I would gladly offer them, and I would also like to offer my whole body for medical research. What is the Church attitude on this?

As Pope Pius XII already pointed out, no one has the right to dispose arbitrarily of our bodies after death and, in so far as it is possible, they should attempt to take our relatives' will and sentiments into account when this will and these sentiments are reasonable.

Still, just as it is morally admissible to sacrifice life or health for the good of our neighbor, it is all the more licit and proper to sacrifice our own dead body for the purpose of research that will promote the good of humanity, especially medical research, which can result in discoveries that will benefit great multitudes of people. Particularly, we might donate the retinas of our eyes, to help in the cure of the blind.

This does nothing to contradict our hope in the resurrection of the body or our appreciation of human dignity.

Christ himself prepared the way for the glory of his resurrection precisely by sacrificing his life upon the cross, in a supreme expression of love of neighbor. Every act of charity increases the glory of our risen body.

Our Savior has said: "He who gives his life for others will find it again." The man who, during this life, spends himself and his health in the service of others thereby honors the masterpiece of God's hands which is his own body and the gift of the risen Christ. And the man who leaves his body after death as a gift for purposes useful and advantageous to humanity extends the exercise of this love beyond his death.

Naturally, those who carry on such studies and research work on dead bodies must treat them with the greatest respect.

23

DOESN'T SEX EXIST FOR MARRIAGEABLE GIRLS AND CELIBATES?

For young and not so young bachelors and unmarried women (sometimes unmarried only as the result of unfavorable circumstances), is sex a non-existent quantity? Hardly. In reading and in conversation, even on good and proper subjects, certain topics are touched upon which spontaneously give rise to a natural reaction and make us feel disturbed. In our confession, must we accuse ourselves of every least disturbance of the flesh in this respect?

An over-anxious concentration on physical excitations of very slight intensity, which afford a certain sensual pleasure and can, on occasion, result in a complete involuntary satisfaction, is a dangerous preoccupation from many points of view. First of all, it is a useless squandering of the energy that the Christian is supposed to pour out, with real joy and magnanimity, in the service of God and neighbor. Then, it is a danger to chastity by constantly focusing attention on this area of human experience and making it too easy to think about habitually. Thus it is actually a cause of many temptations of various kinds. Not only that, but the normal functioning of the psychological reflexes can also be profoundly disturbed. Psychology is familiar with the phenomenon of a "spasmodic expectation," that is, a form of anxiety and nervous preoccupation which, by its very fear of procuring a sensuous excitation or even full sexual satisfaction, actually only succeeds in accomplishing the very opposite of what it intends, and with far greater frequency.

Scrupulous attention in this area and an overly anxious examination of conscience, aimed at precisely establishing whether we might not have, accidentally, voluntarily consented to these things are just as dangerous as the false opinion which holds that it is morally permissible to deliberately provoke sexual release in an effort to get rid of "bad thoughts." Any voluntary and direct intervention in these processes always creates a much more serious disturbance and increases both the psychic and physical difficulties.

Psychic Equilibrium

In the examination of conscience which precedes confession we must also be on guard against probing too scrupulously or too minutely into this area, out of love of purity. Such a practice only serves to disturb psychic equilibrium, by developing an unhealthy concentration on this problem, which, in turn, can only give rise to obsessive thoughts and desires.

On the other hand, such a great preoccupation with the virtue of chastity is more than proper. How, then, are we to form a clear and peaceful judgment, and know whether or not we are still walking along the path of this beautiful virtue, notwithstanding all our thoughts and all our feelings to the contrary?

First we must recall that virtue is an organic whole. The man who wants to be chaste, and grow in chastity, must first make progress simply in the love of God and neighbor, in the practice of justice, in self-control in other fields, and in overcoming every form of selfishness.

In the second place, he must acquire a more and more profound fear and respect for the mystery of marriage and the sublime vocation of celibacy out of love for the kingdom of God. The chastity of the unmarried is also based on this profound respect for marriage and the more noble vocation of virginity. Those who have remained celibate because of circumstances

contrary to their will, can give meaning to their life
only if they will pray and work at understanding the
meaning of celibacy "for the sake of the kingdom of
God." The man who merely puts up with his situation,
and cannot voluntarily accept his bachelor state will
find much greater difficulties in overcoming temptations
against purity. On the other hand, if his heart is filled
with love of God and dedication to his neighbor's welfare, chastity will find a climate much better adapted
to its development.

The Wife of Lot

The man who keeps coming back to temptations
against purity, delving into his semi-deliberate thoughts
and desires in order to decide whether they are voluntary
or not, in order to know whether it was his own doing
that prompted certain physical sensations, etc., is very
much like the wife of Lot, who kept looking back
towards Sodom and Gomorrha, instead of looking straight
ahead, as she had been ordered, and hence was transformed into a statue of salt. It is much better to put
such doubts aside and, in confession, simply say that
we have encountered these difficulties with impure
thoughts and sensations, without being in a position to
establish precisely how far we have consented, telling
the priest that, notwithstanding all this difficulty, we
have the good intention of observing the virtue of
chastity.

This is the decisive point: the good intention of
progressing in all the virtues and, naturally, in this virtue

of chastity. When there is some doubt as to whether a mortal sin has been committed or not, the man who has the general good intention of practicing virtue can approach the Communion rail without first going to confession.

Pope Pius XII has admonished psychotherapists not to make their patients recall the impure experiences of their past life in too concentrated a way, since this experience would only produce new problems for them. This admonition is also valid, obviously for those scrupulous Christians who love to analyze their past experiences, thoughts, and sensations. This is a habit against which we must very carefully guard.

24

HOW CAN YOU CORRECT IMPROPER LANGUAGE?

I am a working girl. I would be very grateful if you could make some remarks in the Famiglia Cristiana *(which is the most widely read Italian Catholic Magazine), aimed at correcting the habits of some women who regularly indulge in slander and gossipy language and broach subjects that would make anyone blush, without being concerned about the fact that their language reaches the ears of children, or young working girls like me, who can easily be scandalized and harmed. I don't think I am the only one who has this opinion, and I would like to invite all the other young ladies of my class to join me in not encouraging such language on the part of these women, or to be afraid of losing their jobs, but rather to make it understood, with tact and delicacy, even if this means nothing more than turning away instead of listening, that language like this is not to our liking.*

The working girl can frequently find herself in a position where she cannot avoid hearing topics discussed, every day, that make her blush, statements that offend against faith, love of neighbor, or some other Christian virtue, in a more or less serious manner. They would like to react, and show their open disapproval, but they are hindered by their fear of offending the people involved and perhaps losing their position.

We make ourselves equally responsible for improper language whenever we give the impression that we approve of it, by the way we act. We offend against the love of neighbor, or whatever virtue it is that is offended against by the words in question, whenever, for an improper reason, we neglect to correct it. This, of course, is not to say that we must correct our neighbor every time he says something that is out of place. This is true particularly when it is a question of weakness or oversight on his part, slight failings that will be corrected even without our interference. Otherwise, our interference might produce just the opposite result, making him angry and provoking him to even more

serious offenses. The problem is precisely in learning
how to tell when correction, in a given circumstance,
will produce better results than mere silence.

Brotherly Correction

The writer of the letter asks, prudently, how it is
possible to discharge the obligation of brotherly correction without alienating the people involved. This
preoccupation is more than justified, and it reminds us
forcefully of another far more important side of the
apostolate of fraternal correction: we must exercise
this obligation in such a way as to make an enemy of
no one, whether our work depends on it or not. The
apostolate is really fruitful only when we succeed in
winning people's hearts. Thus, if the mere concern
about not losing business or risking a job already imposes an obligation to be courteous, discreet, and well-
meaning in our correction of others, this line of conduct
is even more obligatory in terms of making our apostolate
a fruitful one. We must help others in such a way
that they will correct their faults not only when they
are in our presence, but with such tact and delicacy
that they will realize that we are concerned only with
their welfare and are doing them a much more precious
service than merely working in their employ. Fraternal
correction is a real art and it needs to be studied. In
addition to the coarse harshness of simple contradiction,
dishonesty, and direct correction, there are a thousand
other forms as well.

Sometimes a severe or disapproving look is enough,

or, better yet, a look filled with kindness, expressing our sorrow and disappointment at hearing such out of place remarks. It is possible to simply interrupt an out of place conversation, but it is also possible to simply avoid it by cleverly changing the subject or by a touch of humor. Sometimes it is necessary to correct a statement that has caused grave scandal, but perhaps it might be better to do so by using a positive expression which cannot be interpreted as a reproof or personal disapproval. Sometimes it will be absolutely necessary to silence the conversation by direct intervention, which will clearly insult and anger the party in question, but in such a case we must always add at least a good word or two in his regard, and then have a private talk with him to clarify the situation. Love for our neighbor, who might be scandalized by such improper language, does not demand that we show our disapproval directly or immediately, and for that very reason, before saying anything public, it is well to have a private face to face conversation with the party in question.

Good Intentions

When you take a bull by the horns, you generally do not tame him; you make him even more obstinate. Even improper conversation and language almost always contains something good, or at least it starts from a good intention. In such cases, it is better to call attention to the good intentions of the person involved, to establish a spiritual bond with the goodness that is within him, and only then tactfully call attention to what is wrong and improper in his manner of speaking. Such a procedure is always more effective; it wins his heart.

This was the spirit and practice of Pope John. He always looked primarily for what could bind people together, and in this way he worked miracles in breaking down the barriers that divide Christians from other men.

25

IS SMUGGLING A SIN?

*This flood of Capuchin scandals * stems from a mentality that is common not merely to the Capuchins. Many people say that smuggling is not a sin, and act accordingly. I have to laugh at an observation recently made here in Venice. When there were no clerics in the government, some of them said that smuggling was not a sin. But when the clerics entered government, these same men reported the opinion of a German moralist that it is a sin (and apparently agreed).*

If it should prove to be true that certain religious have actually, knowingly, collaborated with an organization of smugglers, receiving their contraband goods

---

* The writer refers to an incident involving contraband cigarettes which took place in the Capuchin monastery at Albano (Rome).

into their silent and out-of-the-way monastery, there would obviously be a very great scandal. But our Lord would probably have an answer for those who recently showed such a willingness to express their anger and contempt: "Let him who is without fault cast the first stone" (John 8, 7). Anyone who takes the presumed or even demonstrated faults of a few men as an excuse to pass harsh judgment on a religious order that is as well deserving as the Capuchins, or all religious for that matter, inevitably needs to face the condemnation of the Teacher who admonished us: "Judge not."

Still, we students of moral theology are not in a position to evade the question as to whether or not some manuals of moral theology share the responsibility for the sad phenomena of smuggling actually carried on by religious monks. What does moral theology actually have to say on this subject? What is the safe solution?

We cannot deny the fact that some manuals do not express themselves with the desired clarity on this point, nor that the statements of various authorities do not agree in every detail. This discrepancy, however, is not to be explained in terms of the fact that some moralists have written under a clerical regime, while others have worked under a non-Christian government. In this respect we need quote only St. Alphonsus de' Ligouri, whose authority in the field of moral theology is universally recognized: he clearly teaches that Christian merchants are bound in conscience to pay the taxes and duties justly imposed by the government, even if the government is made up of non-believers (*Theologia moralis*, III, 615). The classic position on the binding character of the import and duty laws is that of St. Alphonsus: he teaches that, without exception, just import laws, emanating from legitimate authority, oblige in conscience. He also adds that, according to the more common and probable opinion, transgressors are bound to make good the damage they have caused by their transgression.

Most interesting is his lengthy analysis of the various opinions especially since he explains the historical situation in which the various theologians lived and worked. Some authors saw good grounds, in the particular situation of their time and country, for doubting the legitimacy of the customs laws and certain other taxes, since the money collected from them was used almost exclusively to maintain the luxurious living of the many princes, counts, marquis, etc., who stood at the head of so many tiny kingdoms. The customs barriers were actually so high as to be really unbearable. At the same time, the state's censorship on books prevented the theologians from speaking openly and saying that many of their country's customs and tax laws were unjust. That is why their teaching, very prudently, took on the form of a statement that there are some customs laws which do not directly oblige in conscience, but simply impose the obligation of submitting to the threatened punishment without protest, if caught.

Yes, It Is a Sin

By way of conclusion, St. Alphonsus sums up the opinion of those theologians who are less strict in this area: "As a general rule, we must teach people that they are bound to observe all the customs laws; but when a person has transgressed them he cannot be forced to make restitution whenever he has arrived at the conviction, on the basis of solidly probable motives, that he has already paid more than enough customs duties, granted the large number of such taxes that actually exist, or whenever he is convinced that he has already made abundant contributions to public needs, in other areas" (I, quest. 616).

But groups of smugglers, who live and grow rich by organized circumvention of the taxes due to the state, cannot cite a single worth-while theologian in their favor.

In every century, such activity has always been considered as a serious sin against public order and justice.

Basically, the discussions of the moralists were concerned only with the question of whether a person is obliged to pay the customs duty on those objects which he is carrying with him and which are intended for his own personal use or that of his family. We must say, in this respect, that many wise and learned moralists of the 18th and early 19th centuries, faced with the innumerable customs barriers of that time (especially in Italy which was parcelled up into so many tiny states), maintained that customs duties did not oblige in conscience when it was a question of objects intended for personal use, excepting for the case in which the laws, for good and sufficient reasons, expressly included such objects.

St. Alphonsus goes on to say that the poor cannot be

accused of sin in this area, if they have refused to pay the customs duties on goods that are absolutely necessary for maintaining their life; according to the fundamental law of nature a man is obliged to think first of what he needs to support himself and his family, and only then to worry about taxes. But this is not an authorization for poor people to organize into bands of smugglers.

Professional smugglers have never, in any respect, been able to appeal to the opinion of any moralist approved by the Church. Only ignorance and a lamentable inability to make proper distinctions can accuse Catholic morality of favoring the transgression of customs laws, since such action is always harmful to the public good.

It must be admitted that, in its broader outlines, Catholic moral theology has always remained faithful to the principle of St. Paul: "Therefore one must be subject, not only to avoid God's wrath but also for the sake of conscience.... Pay all of them their dues, taxes to whom taxes are due, revenue to whom revenue is due" (Rom, 13, 5-7). She has not ever changed these principles to conform to external circumstances; she has, however, needed to make different applications in terms of the constant and profoundly diverse circumstances of history.

Laws Binding in Conscience

Neither God nor his Church wants us to hide the truth or to tell lies. Thus we must honestly admit that here and there some Catholic moralists merely keep repeating, as if by rote, the solutions proposed by moralists of bygone days, without seeming to realize that formal obedience to their words can only betray their spirit, and the spirit of the Gospel.

Today in a state that is so organized, free, and democratic as Italy is, no one can possibly deny that the customs laws must be considered as just and binding in conscience. Obviously, greater leniency is called for in judging the case of small and insignificant objects, generally intended for personal use, transgressions which the customs officials themselves are regularly inclined to overlook. But smuggling on a large scale, organized smuggling, as well as any collaboration in such an undertaking, is to be judged as a serious transgression, not only with respect to the state or government involved, but also in conscience.

26

WHEN IS OCCULT COMPENSATION JUSTIFIABLE?

A year or so ago, the man I work for, to show his satisfaction with my work, gave me a small raise in salary. Now, one year later, the new boss has decided to take away the extra financial help. When I asked him why, he answered that since the contract was shortly to be renewed,

he had decided to withhold the raise until that
time; there was, he insisted, no other reason.
When I was going to high school, the priest who
used to teach us religion explained to me that
a person can take occult compensation if, for
example, he is not being paid a just wage as he
deserves. Now I would like to know whether
it is all right for me to pick up little things
(pencils, stamps, etc.), in partial compensation
for the loss I have thus incurred. I should like
to add that I am still doing just as much work,
with just as much care, and with great attention
to my employer's interests.

"Occult compensation", like any other ambiguous answer, does not generally represent the normal solution for any difficulty. From the point of view of commutative justice, the case is a simple one: when it is established as certain, for example, that an employer is unjustly refusing to pay an employee or hired man the salary he deserves, the man in question is not violating his employer's rights if he makes this damage good in some other way, by simply securing his own rights in simple justice.

Once these conditions have been verified, the person who has taken occult compensation does not have to make restitution or make anything good to the other party, since he has not violated anyone's rights in justice.

But if we inquire whether or not this form of compensation is actually morally correct in a given case, then the answer is not always so simple, because in such a case, as far as justice in concerned, we need to take other natural and Christian values into account as well.

First of all, the virtue of "probity" demands that we do not act secretly when it is possible to obtain justice by a frank and open explanation. This, for example, might well prove to be one motive, among others, for joining a good union, in order to guarantee a fair wage for ourselves, and for others as well.

In the second place, if we are too hasty in resorting to "occult compensation", we will eventually destroy that mutual trust and faith which is one of the cornerstones of human society. If, for example, those who had recourse to such occult compensation were good Christians, knowledge of the fact that they are easily inclined to practice occult compensation by appropriating other people's property could easily destroy people's trust in them and thus ruin the work of the apostolate. In many cases, thus, it is wise to forego this practice of occult compensation, if only to keep from destroying mutual faith and trust.

In the third place, we must remember how easy it is to be the occasion of false suspicion in this area, thereby offending against love of neighbor, or causing the other party to take counter-measures and make his control even more unbearable.

Fourthly, in many cases, it might well be a "proper degree of self-love" that keeps us from such a course of action, since we would otherwise lose our inner sense of peace.

Finally, we must not forget that when we consider our own case and circumstances, it is easy to be somewhat prejudiced and end up believing that we have a right where actually we do not have one.

In the vast majority of such cases, only a real state of serious necessity, in a situation that is obviously and even notoriously unjust, can excuse the practice of "occult compensation."

27

SUPERFLUOUS GOODS TO THE POOR

I would like to ask for a more exact interpretation of the Gospel passage (Luke 11, 41) in which Christ commands us to give our superfluous goods to the poor. I have the impression that most common explanations are vague, not really exhaustive, and certainly far from convincing. What are we to understand by the term "superfluous goods"?

It is more than justifiable to ask if we might not perhaps have grown accustomed to concentrating too simply upon the concept of almsgiving in considering the disposition of our superfluous goods. For the great Fathers of the Church — the great Christian writers of the first centuries — the point of departure for our duty of love for the poor is not, properly speaking, a theology of superfluous goods; they take great pains to point out that the true Christian, faced with the spectacle of

poverty in his neighbor, cannot, in conscience, regard
his superfluous goods as really being his property. The
point of departure for this question, in classical theology,
is a much different truth, the fact that God, the common
Father of all humanity, has lavished his blessings upon
the earth and endowed individuals with special blessings
for the common benefit of the whole human family; and
that, on the other hand, the principle of private property
is good and right insofar as it represents the best way
to increase the quantity of goods men need and to
achieve the greatest possible production and exploi-
tation of material resources. In the light of these fundamental truths, the Fathers naturally discussed the
concept of superfluous goods. St. Augustine has this
to say: "What is superfluous in the hands of the rich
man is a necessity of life for the poor man; to monopolize
superfluous goods for oneself means to keep someone
else's property for oneself" (*Commentary on the Psalms,*
147, 12). St. Ambrose, Augustine's teacher, once answered a questioner who asked why he should be giving
his superfluous goods to the poor by saying that he was
simply giving back their property to the poor.

Christ's Example

Those who took the preaching on the solidarity of
all humanity in the sight of God seriously, and understood the meaning of earthly goods as gifts of the common Father, had no difficulty in understanding what
these great teachers really meant by superfluous goods.
The man who makes a loyal and serious effort to love

his neighbor as himself and to honor God, the common Father, in his use of the goods of earth, will establish the measure of what is superfluous, not in terms of the conduct and attitudes of the miserly or foolish people in this world, but rather by taking inspiration from Christ, who, though he was infinitely rich, made himself poor out of love for us, and by maintaining a constant awareness of the real needs of other people.

In the later centuries, under the influence of a more individualistic mentality, theologians began to enter into lengthy discussions in an effort to define the concept of superfluous goods. They wrote whole treatises in their attempt to define it precisely, and they laid so much stress on the principle of "requirements suitable to one's state in life," in reference to the higher social classes, that it seemed no one any longer had any superfluous goods to give to the poor, considering the demands of their own rank in society. Pope Innocent XI was forced to condemn the statement that it would be very hard to find a person who actually possessed superfluous goods, beyond the needs of his social level (Denz. 1162).

Solidarity and Brotherhood

The Second Vatican Council has not attempted to establish precise terms for what is or is not to be considered superfluous. In many documents, it recalls the basic solidarity of the whole human race, on every plane, indicating, as the ultimate norm, the solidarity that Christ demonstrated towards every man. It exalted the spirit of poverty, which helps us to understand the true meaning of earthly goods, and it invites everyone to generosity and magnanimity. Every man, whatever his race and nation, is our neighbor whenever we can contribute to alleviating his poverty and need. It is the task of all of God's people, working behind the words and example of their bishops, to alleviate, in the measure of their individual potential and capacity, the misery of our age, by giving, according to the ancient practice of the Church, not only our superfluous goods, but also our necessities of life (Constitution on the Church in the Modern World, 88).

The future of Christianity and the whole world depends, to a large extent, on the nobility of soul and the generosity of those who call themselves Christians. If Communism has asserted itself so strongly and become so dangerous, this has been possible only as a result of the fact that the property owner and influential people in the so-called Christian countries made every possible effort to preserve their material privileges in the face of the needs and aspirations of lower classes, and frequently even appealed to "almsgiving" as a means for continuing to live with their conscience, in their more privileged conditions, while still keeping other people in their position of inferiority. Today, if the classes and peoples who call themselves Christians were to come generously to the support of needy peoples, helping them to develop and increase their natural resources, Communism would lose all its appeal.

28

CAN A MAN WHO HAS AN INNOCENT PERSON CONDEMNED BE AT PEACE WITH HIS CONSCIENCE?

I have been profoundly disturbed by a statement made by a priest, to the effect that no one is ever bound to condemn himself (Nemo tenetur damnare seipsum). We were discussing the case of an innocent person who had been accused and condemned while the guilty party managed to escape justice. According to the priest, the guilty one can go to confession, receive absolution, and go to communion, without being obliged to turn himself in. But surely this cannot be right! How could we possibly be at peace with our conscience if an innocent man has been unjustly punished on our account? Can we say that we have made our peace with God if, after having done something wrong, we commit an even more serious crime in allowing an innocent person to suffer in our place? Either the divine law is not perfect (and this sounds like blasphemy) or else the priest was very wrong in what he told me.

We are always obliged to confess our sins in the sight of God, his saints, and the minister of his Church. This self-accusation, however, is safeguarded by the secrecy of confession and thus does not run the risk of becoming public property. There are, in fact, some well founded reasons for not making our guilt known far and wide.

Thus, even if we have committed a crime, we are not, always and under every circumstance, bound to hand ourselves over to justice; in fact, we are normally not obliged to do so at all, just as we are not obliged to accuse ourselves in a court of law in our modern society. On the other hand, however — and this we must not ever forget — it is never, under any circumstances, allowed to tell a lie or swear a false oath in order to defend ourselves.

In the case that an innocent person is condemned in place of the guilty party, the guilty party has an obligation to do everything he can to change the sentence and set him free. The man who has committed a crime must not only do penance before God but also accept the punishment of men in case he is caught and condemned. He knows that human justice always seeks out the guilty party, and thus the very fact of his crime causes an innocent person to be suspected and, in some cases, also condemned.

Making Good the Injustice

When the judiciary authority is not sufficiently diligent and discerning, and punishes the innocent party, part of the guilt always rests with the judiciary. The real guilty party, however, who has, perhaps, conducted himself under false pretexts, always remains the one who is primarily responsible and it is he who must do everything possible to repair the injustice caused by his offense if he wants to obtain God's pardon, that is, a fruitful and valid absolution in the sacrament of confession. Frequently there will be some other way to inform the judiciary that it has made a serious mistake in condemning an innocent person, and in this case the guilty party cannot be obligated to turn himself in, of his own free will, even though the great grace of a genuine inner conversion could, in just such a case, induce him to give himself up and freely accept the penalty that will make good his offense. When, however, there is absolutely no other way to save the innocent party — from the penalty of death or any other injustice he will have to suffer — then the guilty party has to give himself up, simply because this is the only way to repair the injustice he has caused.

I realize that some moralists have, at times, proposed a different solution. This, however, was largely the result of the fact that they resolved the case, not in the light of moral theology, that is, in the light of God and a genuine interior conversion, but only juridically, in terms of the prevailing human legislation. Such an opinion, however, is not tenable whenever we consider the case in the light of Christ's laws, the law of love and the law of justice — whenever we are concerned with a real conversion of heart.

29

DOES THE NINTH COMMANDMENT UNDER-EVALUATE WOMAN?

*The mere phrasing of the commandment, "thy
neighbor's wife", already implies some sort of
possession. This possession, in my opinion, is
simply something sentimental because even marriage, as a strict biological function, denies the
element of blindly possessive or physiological
possession and belonging. Now, if woman today
has succeeded, effectively, in arriving at full
intellectual equality with man, in the framework
of our modern society, how is it possible for
this commandment to underevaluate her so,
when she demonstrates a possession of truly
estimable values, such as, for example, understanding and self-sacrifice, qualities that are, I
think, less in evidence in the make-up of a man.*

It is true, of course, that the formulation of the ninth
commandment does not cast the same brilliant light on
the concept of woman's dignity as does the figure of
the Blessed Virgin or St. Paul's teaching on marriage,
as developed in the fifth chapter of his Letter to the
Ephesians.

Behind the "formulation" of the Old Testament
commandment — not behind the reality that it was meant
to inculcate — there lurks a certain measure of imper-

fection, the imperfection that is manifest in all the books of the Old Testament, under many other aspects as well. God willed to lead his people to the fulness of truth only gradually. Thus, we must recognize that it was a serious moral failing for the patriarchs and kings of Israel to indulge in polygamy with a peaceful conscience; God did not ever permit it in their case, but long centuries were to pass before the sapiential books of the Old Testament could clearly teach that polygamy was contrary to the dignity of woman and man alike.

Imperfect Vocabulary

Another grave defect in the morality of the Jewish people was to be found in the fact that, for a long time, only the adultery of the woman was punished, not that of the man; this same mentality, incidentally, is reflected, and supported by vigorous arguments, in the laws of some modern states which punish a woman for adultery but absolve the man. This practice obviously presupposes a conception of woman as something owned by the man, and refuses to recognize the fact that woman is equal in dignity to man, and that man is bound to the same fidelity as woman.

Moreover, we must remember that the Mosaic Law was expressed in a vocabulary and style of a people who were morally still quite imperfect, and we who are Christians are somewhat scandalized at seeing how woman is listed among the property and possessions of the man, and defended as such. On the other hand, however, we must also thank God, all the more for this commandment which, long before the coming of Christ, succeeded in educating the Hebrew people, teaching them to look upon adultery in the man on the same plane as in the woman. The formulation of the ninth commandment thus already represents great progress over the original rough customs of the Hebrew people.

We Christians must learn to consider all these things in the fulness of light in Christ. The fulness of the New Law is not expressed in the ninth commandment of the Law of Sinai, but in the Sermon on the Mount, where the Master of all masters teaches us that we offend against the dignity of woman if we even look at her impurely. This is no longer a question of defending the man's rights or a gradual pedagogy in view of a higher form of morality: in the law of Christ we already behold the dignity of God's own image, existing in both man and woman in an equal purity of heart.

30

THE CHURCH'S STAND ON PENANCE AND MORTIFICATION

Doesn't the Church's regulation on abstinence from meat, on Fridays, seem rather absurd? *

* Even though the law of Friday abstinence was revoked in America as of December 2, 1966 — the essential point of Father Häring's answer is, of course, still pertinent.

What is really absurd is the fact that there are some Christians who think they can live their Christianity fully and completely without any element of mortification and self-denial. But it is just as absurd to think that mere Friday abstinence would be enough for this purpose. It is also very annoying to note that in the business of regulating the abstinence legislation, there were in the past so many differences from one diocese to another.

The point made by the objection in the letter could not be made to stand up against the Apostolic Constitution of Pope Paul VI, at the beginning of Lent (1966), in which the penitential tradition of the Church was given a new dimension which partly confirms and partly changes the current discipline.

In reconfirming the threefold form of prayer, fast, and charity as the means to obey the divine commandment of penance, the Constitution stressed the fact that these forms are not exclusive and leave ample scope for the Bishop's Conferences of the individual countries to acquaint the faithful in their care with those external forms of penance which best correspond to the mentality and customs of each individual people.

Thus, even granting the faculties of the individual bishops and pastors to dispense, for a reasonable cause, from the law of abstinence, it is primarily the Episcopal Conference of a given nation who are called upon to regulate the penitential discipline within their respective countries in such a way as to eliminate the disproportions and inequities which have created such confusion in the past.

Beneficial Precept

It is equally important to explore another side of
this question: dispensation from Friday abstinence has
not always represented a genuine benefit. It has also had
unfavorable effects when it became an excuse for no
longer thinking of mortification and self-denial. Considered in itself, the precept of abstinence is beneficial
for us, because it invites us to think, with gratitude and
love, about the passion and death of our Savior, and to
imitate him by self-denial and mortification. Between
the rich man who vacations along the Riviera and completely forgets about Christian mortification, and the
poor man who stays at home and abstains from meat
on Fridays, it is really the poor man who enjoys the
advantage.

The rich man, who does not give up anything at all,
and allows himself to enjoy everything that is possible,
is, in God's sight, in a much worse position than the
poor man who is satisfied with his situation and accepts,
in a truly Christian spirit, all the big and little acts of
self-denial that his state in life imposes on him, even
though he might not always observe the precept of
abstinence perfectly.

In times past, this precept was much more general in
extension and meaning. It was much more rigorous and
it required the renunciation of every form of heavy
eating or special foods. Moreover, throughout the whole
of Christianity it was considered as a public act of worship. Today, on the other hand, the precept has been
mitigated in many respects and in some respects even

abolished. Many regions have obtained a dispensation and, for that matter, even without a dispensation, it is not too hard to procure a really delicious dinner without violating the letter of the law. Such a situation has led Catholic moral theology to take the following steps:

1. to lay greater stress on the spirit of the law.

2. to be more lenient in judging the literal observance of the precept. Today it is easier than it was in times past to accept reasons that excuse from the penitential discipline. If this were not the case, it would be impossible to explain how the Church has become more lenient in giving dispensations. But, on the other hand, the person who holds fast to the literal observance of the precept — for reasons of health, in order to keep the meat from spoiling, etc. — would have to ask himself seriously, in his conscience, whether, in general, he might not really be in a position to make another sacrifice spontaneously. The observance of Friday abstinence is not an absolute and irremovable precept; what is absolute and irremovable, for every Christian, is the need for sacrifice and self-denial.

Might it not, for example, be reasonable for the smoker to give up, or at least cut down, his quota of cigarettes on Friday? Or a person might prefer to abstain, wholly or partially, from alcoholic drinks on Friday. It might be a good substitute to take special pains, on Friday, in our deliberate attention to the needs of other people. For many girls and young ladies, Friday might be a good day to give up a frivolous magazine or movie, and give the money they save to the poor or to the missions.

31

SCHEDULE OF CHURCH SERVICES FOR WORKING MEN

I cannot understand why afternoon Mass is late during the summer and during the winter it is early, as if we workingmen could manage to leave work to go to Church just because it is winter. I would like to know what good it does for Church to be open at four. That's fine for housewives and students, but what about the workingmen?

These questions are very practical ones, and they pose a very important problem. They are phrased in the very concise and objective manner of the workingman. The rhythm of modern living and especially the rhythm of modern work and its demanding timetables and schedules do not follow the traditional habits of the Church which were developed, largely, in an era in which it was country and small-town living that predominated. In these matters, the Church has an obligation to adapt to modern living, and Pope Pius XII already demonstrated the fact that she is aware of this obligation by gladly giving permission for the celebration of Mass in the afternoon and evening, in order to make it possible for everyone to attend the Eucharistic Sacrifice during the week. The Council has sanctioned and confirmed, under every aspect, the justice of this principle.

Still, in every diocese and in every parish, these new principles cannot always be carried out with the same promptness. For that matter, the situation is not the same in all respects. In many country parishes, the rhythm of living is the same as it was a hundred years ago. What is more, in periods of transition, we regularly find a coexistence and intermingling of quite different schedules and forms of life, and thus the situation very often ends up as merely another application of the well-known sociological principle of the status quo, even in the area of religious and Church life. It is easier to keep doing things the way they have always been done without being worked up about it, and without getting up one's courage and introducing new changes. There are, in fact, many Christians who are very pious and obedient as long as their customary rhythm is not disturbed, but who turn into positive rebels as soon as any form of change is threatened. The reasoning runs like this: "What was good enough for my father is good enough for me." The only real problem with this line of reasoning, particularly for the farmer, is the fact that he might meet only failure whereas his father, in his time, was able to reap considerable success with the same method.

I know one diocese outside Italy in which the Vicar General has, as a matter of principle, forbidden the saying of evening Mass, even though it has already been introduced in most other places with the express blessing and recommendation of the Holy See. One pastor,

95% of whose parish is composed of families of working people, had a parish council made up entirely of workingmen. One day they came to see him and told him, quite frankly and openly, that it would be better to obey the Holy Father and make it possible for them to attend Mass in the evening, at least once or twice during the week, on their way back from work at night; in the morning it was impossible for them to go to Church since they worked outside the town and had to leave for work before the first Mass started. The pastor wrote to the diocesan chancery office, explaining the reasons that his parishioners had brought up; the answer was extremely negative and presented this line of reasoning: "Rome would do better not to allow evening Mass at all." This was enough to make him understand whom he should obey, and he decided to follow the Pope and the just requests of his parishioners. Two years later, the bishop came for a parish visit. The first thing the pastor explained was that, for two years now, despite the negative response from the chancery office, he had been celebrating evening Mass at least once a week, and he invited him to attend that very evening if he had the time and the desire. When the bishop saw the church full of working men and women, there were tears in his eyes, and, instead of reprimanding the pastor, he praised him publicly.

Seizing the Proper Opportunity

The lesson to be gained from this — and which is also the only real answer to the letter — is this: workingmen ought to talk to their pastors, and if necessary their bishops, and tell them what their work schedule is and what changes they would like to see in the parish weekly schedule. The Constitution on the Church, as worded by the recent Council, clearly states that the faithful not only have the right, but sometimes even the duty of presenting their needs and their desires to the clergy. This they are to do with "that freedom and confidence that is befitting a child of God and a brother in Christ" (n. 37). The more frequently and the more articulately lay people learn how to explain their points of view to their pastors, always with naturalness and courtesy and not without determination, the more they will be listened to, and the more their requests will be satisfied and taken into consideration.

In this respect, it is most important to take advantage of the right moment to ask. For example, if the pastor has just finished a sermon on the Mass, insisting that everyone take part in the services and consider it as a serious sin to neglect the Sunday precept without very good reason, then that is an excellent time to approach him, after thanking him for the excellent instruction, with a suggestion that the Mass schedule (which would not be too hard to change, would it, Father?) is preventing some 20 workingmen from attending Church, since they are on a shift basis. What about these 20 mortal sins?

For the rest, whenever an atmosphere of trust, cordiality, and reciprocal sincerity prevails in the relationship between pastor and parishioners, a spirit that is evident in the friendly and constant exchange of ideas between them, the laity will not find it difficult to keep their parish up to date with current changes that appear in their individual timetables of work and living conditions, and propose certain modifications in parish schedules and practices that will enable all the members to play an active role.

The Sacraments

32

BAPTISM AND THE USE OF REASON

> By baptism, a human being is transformed into
> a Christian and a new creature. If he is a baby,
> he becomes a Christian without realizing it,
> without any act of his own will, and thus the
> whole ceremony seems rather pointless to me.
> A baby becomes a Jew because his parents are
> Jews, and a baby becomes a Catholic because
> his parents are Catholics and have him baptized
> — not by any exercise of his own free will. This,
> I believe, is precisely why faith has become so
> flat and insipid today: it is without personal
> conviction. Why not wait with baptism until
> the baby is old enough to understand what is
> going on?

Baptism, like the natural life of man, and, for that
matter to an even greater degree, is a free gift from God,

a gift that makes us into his children. Now, just as it is no injustice for God to create us without first asking our consent, even so we can recognize a marvelous evidence of his love in the fact that he calls us to become his children immediately after our entry into this world. Naturally he wants to have children who are free and conscious of their great good fortune and that is why he does not permit his Church — excepting for the case of imminent danger of death — to baptize babies and minors whenever their parents or guardians are not in a position to undertake the responsability of educating them as Christians until the age at which they are capable of appreciating the reality and value of baptism.

A Good Remedy

Still, too many baptized people seem to be in ignorance of what has taken place within them in this sacrament. The remedy for this unhappy situation is not, however, to be found in making the children of Catholic parents wait until the age of reason before receiving the sacrament of baptism, so that they are in a position to appreciate what it means. The answer is rather to be found in the cooperation and devoted activity of all the interested parties. This, concretely, is what we suggest:

1. Baptism should be administered in the presence of the whole parish community. All the parishioners should rejoice with this little baby who is about to become a child of God; they should all sing together,

recite the Creed, and, together, with the child and in his name, repeat the baptismal vows, fully aware of the meaning of the activity that is going on, aware that, by their participation, they bind themselves, before God and his saints, to undertake the Christian education of this child some day, when it has attained the use of reason, and this not only by nice sounding words, but by the shining example of a life of faith.

2. The impending reforms in the baptismal liturgy will make the ceremony even more meaningful, since even little children, at the age of five or seven, will be able to share, fruitfully, in the administration of the sacrament, as well as to recognize and more profoundly feel the great joy and honor of knowing that they are baptized children of God.

3. In a particular way it must be the family and relatives who take part in the rite and make a greater effort to understand the unfathomable treasure which our Savior has given to their newborn child, right from his cradle. Thus they will be more and more conscious of the fact that, from this moment on, their home and their education must have one single purpose, to guard this treasure and bring it to its gradual maturity.

4. Christianity must not be understood and presented primarily as a law or a complex of laws, but rather as a grandiose and sublime way of life in Christ; in such a way it will also be much easier to see the law of Christ as it really is, that is, as the joyous message of our dignity and privilege of divine sonship.

33

IS IT POSSIBLE THAT GOD MIGHT NOT FOR-GIVE US?

A priest once assured me that it is a dogma of our faith that the sins we confess with the proper dispositions are forgiven before God, in every case, with absolute certainty. Also, that the proper dispositions depend on both our own free will and a grace from God which we call "sufficient grace," — it being also a dogma of faith that God gives this grace to "all men, in every instant" of their life, up to the moment of death. If this is the case, then any man, even a man who is responsible for very many serious crimes, can not only hope in the mercy of God but, after having confessed his own sins, he can be "most certain" of being forgiven by God. Is this really true?

There are two questions in this letter, and they must be kept distinct. The first one concerns the certainty of our sins being forgiven, while the second wants to know whether God actually gives every man, at every moment of his life, this "sufficient grace" that he requires.

a. If we have sincere purpose of abandoning our sinful habits and honestly confess them, we can be sure that God will pardon them. This also holds for the case of the individual who is so perplexed or confused in his manner of expressing himself that he is not always able to say everything with the required precision, and even forgets some things.

What really counts, and what constitutes the really decisive element on our part, is simply the honest and forthright intention of confessing our sins in the sight of God. It is true that in this whole process the most important element is the grace that comes from God. In the sacrament of penance, however, we can always be certain that he will be present and at work within us. It is God himself who, through the mouth of the priest, his human instrument, produces the infallible efficacy of his words within us: "Your sins are forgiven." As far as God is concerned, and his mercy and faithfulness, there cannot be even the least bit of doubt.

The only question we might ask here — a question that can perhaps be sometimes resolved with absolute certainty — is this: is my good will really sincere? Am I really intent on doing everything I can and in asking, in my prayers, for whatever is at the moment beyond the reach of my power and will?

b. If we ask steadfastly, God will give us his sufficient grace, the efficacious grace of final perseverance and a happy death. This is a truth which is clearly revealed, a dogma which St. Alphonsus has so marvelously commented on and explained in his book on the great means of prayer. No one is ever denied the grace of prayer.

Still, it is not possible to say, for certain, that God gives this sufficient grace to every man, at every moment of his life. The man who stubbornly rejects the grace of God and especially the grace of prayer, gradually shuts himself out from the light of faith, from the warmth and clarity of grace. Man cannot dare to be capricious in his use of grace. That is why we are admonished: "Today, if you hear his voice, do not harden your hearts" (Ps. 94, 8). The man who, by his ill will or by his slothfulness, stands in the way of his own conversion, places himself in the most serious danger.

Still, even though a man has committed the most serious of sins, or an unbelievably great number of sins, if he prays with sincerity and humility, he has no reason to doubt the mercy of God. The simple fact that he prays with sincerity already means that God has turned towards him with a look of mercy and has come half-way to meet him with his grace, to work his salvation.

34

MASS ABSOLUTION AT EASTER AND CHRISTMAS?

I cannot believe that Christmas and Easter confessions are good confessions. All that crowd in the confessionals, all the rush and hurry, and the poor priests so tired. Frankly I feel that it is confessions such as this that give religion a bad name. Wouldn't it be much better to give a general absolution as is the practice — or so I remember reading — in the case of soldiers during wartime, and then oblige them to confess

*their sins calmly and unhurriedly during the
following weeks?*

The letter asks a pastoral question which is a thorny
one, and of great importance for the whole Church.
Some 150 years ago, Johann Michael Sailer, the famous
moralist and later bishop of Ratisbon, already wrote
that the hurried confessions which take place on certain
days and seasons of the year "cry out to the ears of the
Soverign Pastor of the Church, pleading for a remedy."
Confession of sins and the genuinely personal manifestation of reconciliation and another new beginning along
the never-ending path of conversion or progress are
matters of no little importance. But hurried confessions,
in which the penitent hardly has enough time to speak
and the priest has to be satisfied with one or two words
of encouragement and instruction, confessions in which
even the absolution is hurried over and pronounced
in an unintelligible manner — this does not correspond
to the dignity of the sacrament.

Drastic Solution

The letter, however, suggests a rather drastic solution. For my part, I think that we should make an
effort to get around the inconvenient elements while
still remaining within the framework of the existing
legislation. The first point we might make is to refer
to the case of those pious people who confess very
frequently. It would be well if these could be persuaded
to go to confession only when there is no large crowd.

They generally do not have any mortal sins to confess, and they might be doing a real service by refraining from the confessional on the occasion of big-feast days. They can confess a week before or after, with much greater fruit, and they can still go to Communion on the feast days. Priests too, in their turn, can also make a contribution to the solution of the problem by creating more and more opportunities for the faithful to confess and organizing the parish schedule in such a way as to attend to as many of the faithful as possible during the weekdays.

Still, in my judgment, the proposal contained in the letter is not, in itself, completely out of place. The Church always has the power to introduce such changes into her sacramental legislation, in keeping with the needs and demands of pastoral theology. In many parts of the world, the scarcity of clergy is so acute that even the faithful who have great good will cannot possibly find a priest to whom they can confess their mortal sin, and are thus obliged to do without Communion on Sunday. This clearly represents a serious disadvantage. Faced with such a situation, we need not wonder if, in the future, the Church authorities might not have to introduce the practice, in some territories poor in clergy, of permitting a general absolution, to be given several times a year, imparted to all those who sincerely repent of their sins and desire to go to Communion as soon as they possibly can. This namely that they make an honest effort to get to confession before or during the next Easter Duty Season, and if they have any mortal sin on their soul they must mention it expressely in their individual confession.

We must pray for means to discover a way that will enable all Christians of good will to receive the Body of our Savior every Sunday in the parish celebration of Holy Mass. The Eucharist is the center of our life. In the countries of Western Europe this should be possible almost everywhere, even with the situation as it actually exists. No Christian on Sunday should deprive himself deliberately of his opportunity to participate in the sacrifical banquet of the Eucharist, not even in the case in which he doubts whether he has committed a mortal sin. In such circumstances, as a matter of fact, when he does not have any occasion to go to confession, it is enough for him to repent and make a firm purpose of amendment and then take Communion with a quiet conscience. When he simply doubts that he is in the state of grace or not, the Church does not mean to exclude him from Communion, and his reception of the sacrament is certainly not unworthy, so long as he has managed to elicit sentiments of at least imperfect contrition in his heart, and has made a firm intention of living like a Christian.

35

THE RARE CASE IN WHICH IT IS MORALLY IMPOSSIBLE TO GO TO CONFESSION (I)

I have been told that in some particular circumstance it is all right to pass over even a mortal sin in confession without thereby committing a sacrilege. Is this true?

The Church, further defining the precepts of God's Ten Commandments, prescribes that a person who is aware of having committed a mortal sin must go to confession before receiving Communion. Still, this precept is not a law of nature, that is, one of the commandments that God has written into the heart and spirit of man, obliging absolutely and without any exception. The precepts of the Church admit of exception. Thus, for example, the person who, for all his good intentions, is unable to find a priest to confess his sins during the Easter Season can, and should, still go to Communion even without confessing, even if he is aware of having committed a mortal sin. It is enough for him to sincerely repent, before receiving, and make a serious intention of going to confession at the very first opportunity — at least by the next Easter Season. Similarly, the person who habitually lives his Christian life seriously and with dedication, and who nevertheless has committed a mortal sin and cannot find an opportunity to confess it, since he would suffer from having to go without

Communion for a long time, is free to receive, even outside the Easter Season, provided, of course, that he sincerely repent of his sin and have the intention of confessing it as soon as possible.

Particular Cases

Occasionally the case might be something like this: a person has committed a particularly shameful sin and has no opportunity to confess it excepting to a priest with whom he comes into daily social contact. In this situation, his shame and fear might be so great as to make him psychologically incapable of telling his sin to the priest in question; he might also fear that courageous and sincere confession would result in disturbing the social relationship with the priest because of the psychological complexes that would arise. Sometimes, of course, such a person would be obliged to confess to that priest anyhow, notwithstanding all the above considerations, since his failure to do so, habitually, would not make a good impression and would cause suspicion. In this and similar cases it is morally admissible to approach the sacrament of penance, deliberately omitting the mention of those sins which are particularly shameful. Obviously, the penitent must be sorry for them as well, before confessing his other sins, and he must have the firm intention of mentioning them in a later confession, as soon as possible, before a different priest.

Such an incomplete confession — presupposing that

all the other conditions are fulfilled — is good and fruitful.

The reception of the sacrament of penance, with the proper dispositions, infallibly, with the grace of God, remits our sin and allows us to approach the Communion table. The fact that we are firmly decided to confess these mortal sins to another priest, at least provided we have an opportunity, shows that we are properly disposed towards the commandments of God and the precepts of the Church as well, which are a juridic precision upon the general commandment. In my opinion, it is better to receive the sacrament of confession in this manner than to be satisfied with a mere act of contrition, since the worthy reception of the sacrament is something more than a simple effort at eliciting the necessary dispositions of sorrow in our heart, without recourse to the confessional.

36

THE RARE CASE IN WHICH IT IS MORALLY IMPOSSIBLE TO GO TO CONFESSION (II)

I have just read your article entitled: "The rare Case in which it is morally impossible to go to Confession" (I), signed by Fr. Bernard Häring. How can such a widely read review as yours, with its millions of readers, possibly publish such terrible heresy as that? I can hardly imagine

*the protests, the scandal to good Christians, and
the malicious smiles of the sophisticated! The
good of souls demands a forthright statement of
clarification, published in your forthcoming is-
sues, openly admitting the great mistake you
have made.* Sapientis est mutare consilium! *It is
the mark of a wise man to change his mind!
And please don't try to hedge on the question,
the way you journalists are so good at doing!*

The proper understanding of the precepts of the
Church, that is, the appreciation of their benevolent and
loving intention, is a very important achievement for the
Christian, because the understanding necessarily deter-
mines the attitude he will have towards them.   The
Church is a good mother, with eyes for human weakness
and infirmity.   If Aristotle already teaches, on the subject
of human legislation, that the human lawgiver must
provide for particular cases in which the laws he makes
will not oblige in certain extraordinary circumstances,
we must be all the more willing to suppose this fact of
the Catholic Church.   Her precepts are always directed
towards what is best.   What she desires and attempts
to achieve is not an external and forced obedience, bar-
racks style, but rather an obedience that is born of an
appreciation of her benevolent intentions.   When her
precepts are understood rightly, then they are also
loved and more easily kept with real joy.   The words
of Christ "My yoke is sweet and my burden is light"
(Matt. 11, 30) apply not only to the Commandments of

God, but also to the precepts of the Church, properly understood.

Thus, for example, a Catholic who is properly familiar with Christian doctrine, knows that the precept of attending Mass is not aimed at crowding Catholics together in Church on Sunday, for an hour, for a purely external assistance at the Eucharistic celebration, without any interior participation at all. The man who understands what a great honor and privilege it is to be able to participate in the Eucharistic mystery would go to Church freely and with real willingness, even if the Church did not prescribe it under pain of serious sin. We understand the meaning of this obligation imposed upon us under pain of sin only if we have learned how to appreciate the real value of Sunday Mass.

Divine Precepts

We do the Church an injustice when we illustrate only the external fulfillment of her precepts by the faithful, entirely passing over the deeper meaning that they have. And we do her a real injustice when we do not teach the faithful to distinguish between absolute natural divine precepts, which are always binding, and Church precepts which are binding only under certain conditions. A person who tends in this direction, either immediately smells a "heresy" in what is only a simple matter of opinion — an opinion, for that matter, held by so famous a teacher as St. Alphonsus — or else he clearly shows that his faith is not very enlightened. Just as we are obliged to distinguish truths of faith from simple opinions, and to distinguish heretical statements from some author's personal views which we do not happen to share, we must also be willing to distinguish between the absolute and immutable demands of morality and simple ecclesiastical or divine positive precepts which, no matter how serious and important they may be, are always binding only under determined conditions.

For example, there can never be any grounds that make divorce just or licit, or immorality, or hatred for our neighbor. On the other hand, the mother who does not go to Mass on Sunday because she cannot leave her sick child at home alone certainly does not commit any sin, because the Church cannot have meant to include this extraordinary case in its commandment. The precept of confessing all our mortal sins, committed after baptism, to a priest in the sacrament of penance is a positive precept of God. "Positive" is not to be understood, in this context, as opposed to "negative", but rather in the sense of a regulation or institution freely "posited" or placed in effect by God himself and in addition to the laws of nature. In this institution, too, we should recognize the great gift of Christ who is not content with having the sinner forgiven within the secrecy of God's mystery, but also furnishes him with a tangible, efficacious, and infallible sign of his forgiveness. Correspondingly, the true Christian cannot be so arrogant and niggardly as to calculate, ingeniously, all the possible cases in which it is possible to avoid going to confession to a priest. Still, the Church and her theology teach us that we must make the proper distinctions among the various wise and beneficent norms proposed for our conduct by our divine Legislator, and that, when we are dealing with positive precepts, there are reasons and circumstances which can dispense from their observation.

The divine precept is aimed, in every case, at achieving the good of the human person. That is why God does not mean to oblige in this absolute manner, in those exceptional cases in which the commandment cannot be observed without very serious disadvantages and a certain degree of frustration.

Precepts of the Church

This reasoning is all the more true when applied to the precepts of the Church. Most of the time they are meant to further determine a divine positive precept, to make it more precise, as, for example, the precept of hearing Mass on Sunday, or confessing a mortal sin no later than during the following Easter Season. According to many theologians, the precept of confessing all mortal sins before receiving Holy Communion is also only a precept of the Church. It is the result of the Church's pastoral love for her children. We neglect or deny its beneficent character whenever we make it overly stern and unyielding, as do the Jansenists.

If we really understand its meaning, we are not scandalized or shocked to learn that, according to all the Catholic theologians who have considered the subject, the Church recognizes a whole list of cases which can dispense from its observance. While we cannot ever approve of the desire to get rid of one's sins as quickly as possible — without the true spirit of penance and faith — a proper understanding of the Church's law requires that we see how comprehensive Catholic theology has been in its explanation of this obligation.

Mere shame or humiliation, such as always accompany the confession of any sin, are certainly not sufficient excuse. Still, there can be cases in which the penitent experiences a really extraordinary sense of shame, not because the sin involved is shameful in itself (although that is always an underlying factor), but because of some other extraordinary circumstance. Think, for example, of the father who takes his whole family to confession Saturday evening, so that they can all receive Communion together on Sunday morning. Then, next morning, he realizes that he has committed a mortal sin, by thought, and cannot possibly go to confession again without his wife and children noticing the fact and being able to surmise the reasons behind it. In such a case he may simply put his trust and faith in the Church's understanding and, after having made as perfect an act of contrition as possible, he may freely approach the Communion rail. If he receives Communion with a peaceful conscience, even if his sorrow is only imperfect — for God alone knows this — the reception of Communion itself will, infallibly, put him into the state of grace. In so acting, he is not motivated by a false sense of self-love or any other unworthy reason. Moreover, he means to confess his sin, with all humility, as soon as it is possible.

Integrity in Confession

We can do the same with respect to the integrity of our confession. Think of the case of the person who has committed a shameful sin, and, upon entering the confessional, discovers that the priest is his brother, his uncle, or some other priest with whom he has to deal every day. In such a case, a really integral confession would mean simply an extraordinary act of humiliation. When a person is psychologically sound, a good humiliation does him no harm. But in this case, it would also involve losing the necessary ease and security in social relationships with the priest for a long period of time. Then too although it would be a very rare case — the priest himself might be disturbed and embarrassed at the prospect of further social dealings. Omitting the mention of such a sin, in a case like this, with the intention of confessing it later to a different priest, is not contrary to the positive precept of the Church; it is, rather, a full recognition and intelligent fulfilment of the Church law, and a demonstration of humility and deference.

Moralists have been considering these cases for centuries. Is there any reason to fear, perhaps, that the faithful will be harmed by knowing how good and undertanding the Church is in imposing and interpreting her precepts, and in learning how to distinguish what are the absolute demands of the moral law and what are simply matters of positive precept? As a matter of fact, this is a knowledge that is demanded of the Christian in our modern world: he needs to learn how to make these distinctions. Our conscience is formed in a truly Christian manner, in the sight of God and the Church, only to the extent that it is a faithful echo of the words of our Lord: "No longer do I call you servants, for the servant does not know what his master is doing; but I have called you friends, for all that I have heard from my Father I have made known to you" (John 15, 15). A genuine and accurate awareness of the loving plans of God and the mild burden of the Church's legislation will not serve to make Christians lazy or superficial, but will rather make them more responsive, filled with joy and zeal for the good, the whole good.

37

ARE LAY PEOPLE "PRIESTS" TOO?

I would like to know something about this "royal priesthood." When does the Christian receive it? And how is he to live it in his daily life?

This is a question that every Catholic needs to ask himself today, particularly if he has any interest in the proceedings of the recent Council. Actually, the Council does have a lot to say about this revealed truth which has been all but forgotten by the Christian people. In the third chapter of the schema on the Church, before considering the hierarchical priesthood of the episcopate, priesthood, and diaconate, it calls attention to the doctrine according to which the Christian people, that is, all the members of the Mystical Body of Christ, are signed with the sign of Christ's priesthood, since they are members of him, the Head of the Body; Jesus has chosen and formed for himself a whole people of priests and kings, to the honor of God the Father.

Being a member clothed with the dignity of royal priesthood means this: being united to Christ and his Bride (the Church), not for our own individual honor, but for the honor of God: it means praising and blessing God in everything; cooperating in the salvation of souls, so that all mankind may be united in the universal praise of the triune God. All this is possible only because Christ has deigned to make every Christian a partaker in his priestly mission. Sharing in this "royal priesthood" represents a magnificent elevation of human nature, an ineffable privilege, and, at the same time, a very serious obligation.

In addition to this, our Savior has called some individuals in a particular way to share in the hierarchical priesthood as bishops, priests, and deacons, and has endowed them with particular gift and powers, so that they will render a universal service to all mankind and make humanity fully aware of their participation in the priesthood of Christ and in his mission.

Baptismal Character

The Christian becomes a sharer in this royal priesthood first of all, and fundamentally, by the reception of baptism. The baptismal character confers upon him both the power and the obligation of being united with Christ, the High Priest, and the whole people of God in the praise of our Savior, by living a holy life every day and by sharing in the other sacraments, as well as the power and duty to cooperate in the redemption of humanity. Confirmation adds new strength and vigor to the baptismal character, gives the fulness of the Spirit, makes the Christian brave in confessing his faith publicly and, so to speak, officially, giving public honor to God, even with the ultimate decision of giving one's life for Christ, if the occasion demands. The sacrament of penance purifies the Christian of his sins which constitute an impediment to living his life in true union with Christ, the High Priest, and makes him more worthy and better disposed to live a life of praise of God. Active participation in the Eucharistic sacrifice represents the high point of the exercise of this royal priesthood. The anionting of the sick signifies the intimate conformation of the sick Christian with Christ: thus his humble and tranquil acceptance of his sickness and even of the prospect of death takes on the value of the sublime act performed by Christ upon the cross.

The fourth chapter of the Constitution on the Church explains how it is possible to live this royal priesthood in one's daily life. It says, for example: "All their works, prayers, and apostolic endeavors, their ordinary married and family life, their daily work, times of relaxation and recreation, provided they are all activities performed in union with the Holy Spirit, including every hardship and suffering that is patiently accepted — all of these become spiritual sacrifices acceptable to God through

the intercession of Jesus Christ, a sacrifice devoutly offered
to the Father in the Eucharistic celebration together
with the Body of the Savior" (n. 34).

This text, and other texts, make it clear that the
exercise of the royal priesthood of all the faithful is not
an activity which merely runs parallel to living; quite
the contrary, the Christian is sanctified and made to
share in the priesthood of Christ himself precisely
because he sanctifies his life; and by his life, his goodness,
the fulfillment of his professional duties, his good qualities, his patience with others and with himself, he gives
glory to God and cooperates in the redemption of the
world. He is not to approach the Eucharistic sacrifice
with empty hands; he must conform his living to the
Eucharistic ideal in such a way as to be perfectly united
with the sacrifice of Christ and the Church. Participation in the Eucharistic sacrifice and intimate union with
our Savior in Communion give everyone the capacity to
recognize the will of God in the ups and downs of
everyday living, and the strength to glorify him in all
things.

38

CAN SATAN BE THE CAUSE OF "GRACES"?

*I am a very happy and fortunate person. This
good fortune I owe to God, because he has
always been my guide, and whenever I have*

begged for anything with fervor he has always granted it to me. Now a person who is a member of the Jehovah's Witnesses tried to tell me that the devil can also grant special favors. Now the graces I received were not getting rich or having a good time, or anything like that. Is it really true that Satan can grant spiritual favors? For my part, I requested them from God and it is God to whom I am grateful for them.

The very manner in which this question is put is already an excellent example of the so-called "discernment of spirits", a problem which has always played a fundamental role in the history of moral theology. When a person prays for what the Apostle Paul calls "the fruits of the Spirit," that is "love, joy, peace, patience, kindness, goodness, faithfulness, gentleness, self-control" (Gal. 5, 22), and his prayer is answered, then he can be certain that the grace has come from God. The man who bases his happiness and good fortune in God and finds his joy primarily in God's love and wants to share this joy with other people as well, will, in turn, receive the gift of interior peace from our Savior, a peace which gives him real security in living in God's love.

When, on the other hand, a person is interested primarily in wealth and the pleasures of life and his prayers are "heard" and granted, this is no proof that he has found favor with God. The devil might also be very much interested in such a person's being heard, so that he will learn to depend upon his wealth and become self-centered and secure, gradually coming to forget the love of God.

Wherever there is a preoccupation with human greed and self-seeking — especially "immorality, impurity, licentiousness, idolatry, sorcery, enmity, strife, jealousy, anger, selfishness, dissension, party spirit, envy, drunkenness, carousing, and the like" (Gal. 5, 19-20) — then man, of his own doing, shuts out the Kingdom of God and becomes the victim of the deceitful maneuvers of the devil.

Such temptations can frequently come upon us; the devil acts subtly and ingeniously, taking advantage of the existence of genuine graces such as, for example, the grace of ardent and fervent prayer, tempting us to vanity and inspiring a sense of confidence in our own selves. True grace never comes from the spirit of darkness, but always and only from God. All the inordinate desires and affections which place a man in danger of making himself the center of things, do not come from him alone: they are also a matter of interest and concern to the "father of lies."

Eternal Life

39

IS IT BETTER NOT TO BE BORN OR TO BE BORN AND GO TO HELL?

I once heard in a sermon that God has given us an immense blessing in the gift of human life, and that it is better to be condemned to hell than not to have life at all. I think, rather, that it is better not to have life at all than to be born and go to hell. I would also like to know whether or not children who die without baptism will get into heaven at the end of the world; I am a mother of several children who died without baptism.

With reference to Judas Iscariot, the man who betrayed him, Christ said that it would have been better for him if he had not ever been born. Actually, what good is there in the bare and simple fact of existence, deprived of every positive value, reduced to hatred and the negation of all goodness? What good is there in existing, if it implies a contempt and rejection of everything that makes up the joy of existence, that is, God, his love and his happiness?

Still, from a social and religious point of view, the existence of the condemned in hell still has some meaning: for all eternity they are forced to recognize that God has loved them and willed their happiness; that Christ, the Redeemer of all mankind, died for them too and has offered them all the riches of redemption; they are a constant witness to the fact that God has not willed to save man without his cooperation, nor to make him happy without his own free will. They represent one part of the mystery of human freedom, precisely insofar as they have freely shown their contempt and rejection for the true freedom of the children of God. For all eternity they will bend their knees and confess that Christ is the Lord, the Redeemer, and the Savior who died for all, and this very fact will constitute their eternal punishment as well, since in this way they will be admitting that they alone are the ones responsible for their own sad lot. No one is ever condemned without his own personal and very serious fault.

With respect to the eternal fate of children who die without baptism, the Church has no specific dogma. It is, on the other hand, most true that Christian parents have a serious obligation to have their children baptized as soon as possible.

Baptism endows the child with an incomparable wealth that he could not otherwise possess. On the

other hand, we also know that Christ has died for all
men, even for those children who die before they are
baptized through no fault of their own. The grace and
love of Christ are more powerful and they touch upon
an area of reality which is much vaster than Adam's
original sin. In heaven we will praise our Savior for
the love he has shown to all men, even towards our
children who die without being baptized. Only then
will we see and understand the ways and measure in
which God has made available to them the fruits of his
redemption. For now it is enough for us to know that
God is love and that he acts with infinite and perfect
love towards all his creatures. All who have not deliberately rejected this love, in a total and final act of refusal,
will live upon it in a state of blessedness for all eternity.

40

WILL WE LOVE OUR DEAR ONES EVEN IF THEY ARE IN HELL?

*If, in the hereafter, we have close friends and
relatives in hell, how will our souls react to
them? Could our souls be the same, even if our
loved ones were forgotten?*

Christ loved all men to the point of pouring out his
blood for them, and still he loved his Mother with a
greater love than he had for all the rest. Among the

Apostles, there were three he preferred above the others: Peter, James, and John. Even in heaven, he has given a greater honor and glory to his Blessed Mother. All this, however, does nothing to diminish the happiness of the blessed; in fact it actually constitutes a motive and further object of their joy. Every genuine love on this earth is complemented in heaven in a marvelous and wonderful way, in the love and joy one finds in God, our center and source. Heaven is not a dull existence, buried in the contemplation of God. In the warm and luminous sea of divine love even the love that the saints and blessed have for each other attains its most intense degree. The love we have for our neighbor today, and the love we have for our close friends and relatives, brings us very close to God and the blessedness of his love. In the same way, the beatifying love of God brings us closer and closer to each other as well, in a new and wonderful way, a way we cannot ever possibly imagine here on earth.

This state of affairs, however, poses a new question: if the love that joins us together here on earth is not lost in heaven, but rather brought to its perfection, what will be our attitude towards those whom we have loved on earth and who are, in eternity, everlastingly damned and shut out of the blessedness we know in paradise, and from the love of God? This is a deep mystery. Only by looking to our Savior can we hope to find a satisfactory answer at all: He, the Son of God, poured out all his blood for love of us. He suffered to the point that his sorrows wrung from his lips the agonizing cry: "My God, my God! Why have you forsaken me?" It

was as if the beatifying love of God were veiled from him,
prevented from being manifest in his humanity, so that
he could suffer death. What violent pain there was,
for Christ in that kiss of Judas. He would not have
suffered so much if his hand had been cut off.

Now, however, after the resurrection, he no longer
suffers. We have an obligation, on our part, to unite
ourselves with his suffering and, by our participation in
his passion, to do what we can to keep men from the
fate of hell.

When he returns and leads those who are on his
right hand into the kingdom of eternal happiness, those
who are on his left hand will be separated by an un-
bridgeable abyss. God has no further need of them. He
has sought them in love, but they have rejected him.
He has made man and suffered for them. But, both
as God and as man, he is infinitely happy even without
them.

We too, if we are saved, will be transformed into
complete conformity with Christ. The sufferings of
life which we have endured in order to preserve others
from hell, will all be redeemed and transfigured in blessedness. Once we have entered into heaven, we can
only rejoice and exult perfectly in God. We shall see
and love all things directly in him, in his love and
blessedness. Everything that might possibly cast a
shadow on our happiness will be infinitely removed
from us forever. All the souls of all the redeemed, and
particularly those who have benefitted from our cooperation in their redemption, will be a secondary and
additional source of joy. The damned, on the other

hand, those who are forced to recognize, eternally, the fact that they have deliberately rejected the gift of love and happiness by their own fault, will not disturb our paradise in any way.   Before their minds they will constantly have the spectacle of the mortal sadness suffered by Christ on the Mount of Olives, and they will admit that "He has loved us infinitely and has willed our happiness."   In the same way they will necessarily recognize everything that we have done to bring them closer to God.

Basically, however, we must admit that these truths are too sublime and full of mystery for our human understanding. In respect to them we can only stammer. Only in eternity can we understand how all this is possible.

41

IS IT EASIER FOR CHRISTIANS OR FOR PAGANS TO GET TO HEAVEN?

In a recent discussion with a classmate of mine, I maintained that it is better to be a Catholic: it is harder for pagans to be saved, even though the laws of God (that is all the Ten Commandments) are written on every human heart, so that even pagans can come to know them. But the point was made that it is really much easier for pagans to be saved, since — according to

my opponent — not knowing the true religion,
they do not have the obligations that it implies;
it is thus enough for them to follow the natural
laws of conscience, and even these laws only in
general outline, which is to say that they need
only to avoid the more serious evils, such as not
committing murder, etc.; for the rest, they do
not experience any remorse of conscience either.
Who is right, my classmate or I? Is it easier
for a person who has the grace of the true faith
to get to heaven, or for a person who is still a
pagan?

We set out upon the wrong path whenever we
attempt to settle this question by thinking only of the
laws and obligations which are concerned. The Catholic faith and the way of salvation are not primarily or
solely a law and the fulfillment of a law. Salvation
comes from faith, and faith is an answer to the good
tidings of the Gospel. The law of Christ is contained
in the Gospel as in a joyful message, and thus faith
too is a joyous response to the joy-producing message
of salvation in Jesus Christ and the "law of faith."

For a Catholic it is easier to attain salvation, since
he possesses the fulness of the Gospel message handed
down to him through the agency of the Church in an
authentic and integral way, naturally supposing that he
lives a true Catholic life and opens his heart and his
mind to the voice behind this message. The man who
recognizes the Gospel for what it is cannot help being
filled with joy and gratitude.

Our strength to advance along this way of salvation is the joy of recognition and our gratitude.

The more fully a person understands, by his participation in the Eucharist and the other sacraments, by his constantly more profound awareness of Christ and his teaching and by his faithfulness to the law, that it is a great good fortune to be a Catholic, the easier it will become for him to respond with joy and generosity to all the most sublime demands of his faith. When, on the other hand, his faith and the joy of that faith are reduced to a minimum level, then even its most insignificant demands become something hard to bear.

The Catholic, moreover, not only has a more exact awareness of the joyful message of the Gospel and the law contained in it; he also shares in the salvific community, enjoys the sure guidance of the Church, the direction of her priests, and the stimulating example of the true faithful. Above all, he is confident that Christ has granted him the gift of the life of grace. It is enough for him to want to live according to this supernatural life and he will never be lacking for the necessary help from God.

The Love of Christ Impels Us

The Church is not primarily charged with the execution of the law; she is the Church of the sacraments and the joy of faith. Awareness of this fact confers an extraordinary efficacy upon the preaching of the law. "The love of Christ impels us."

Pagans too can be saved since Christ died for them as well. They are saved, not in virtue of their own good works, but in virtue of the death and resurrection of Christ. This redemption is efficacious in their respect in terms of the faith they have in God, conceived of as the rewarder of good and evil. The good they do must, however, have God as its final purpose and goal, if they want to be saved. Naturally we cannot know for certain the precise measure to which this faith needs to be formulated in a reflex and conceptual manner. The only certain thing is that without faith no adult person can be saved and that faith also includes a firm adherence to the will of God.

Now, since pagans have only a very imperfect knowledge of the love of God and do not experience the full joy of salvation, they are actually in a much worse situation than that of the well instructed Catholic.

On the other hand, we cannot deny the fact that a Catholic who thinks and believes that he can make his way into heaven at the least possible price, thus limiting himself to the indispensable minimum in his knowledge of the faith and his observance of the moral law, is in a very dangerous position. Compared to him, the pagan who does his best to discover the divine will and fulfill it as perfectly as he can is in an advantageous position: in terms of his interior dispositions he is much closer to Christ and to his Church than the mediocre Catholic described above.

In conclusion, if we compare the good Catholic with the good pagan, it is obvious that the Catholic will never be sufficiently grateful to God, since it is easier for him not only to arrive at salvation, but even to live a holy life.

Vocation and Holiness

42

PRIESTS AND THE VOW OF POVERTY

1. What exactly is the "vow of poverty"? 2. What religious take this vow? 3. Do all priests take this vow of poverty, and if not why not?

The members of the classic orders and the religious congregations (such as the Jesuits, the Franciscans, the Salesians, etc.), in addition to their vow of chastity and celibacy for the love of the kingdom of heaven and their vow of obedience to their religious superiors, also take a vow of poverty. The contents of this vow, however, is not the same in all these orders and congregations. There are some orders which restrict the lawful possession of property to a minimum, even as regards the religious community as such, whereas others place no limits on the number and quantity of possessions, which naturally are to be used for spiritual and apostolic purposes. For all religious, the vow of poverty means this: (1) greater and greater detachment from the goods of this earth, (2) renunciation of the right to freely dispose of property (in the orders, this also includes a renunciation of the right to our private property), (3) the obligation of a "common life," that is, the obligation to give over to the community everything that comes to them as the fruit of their own effort or as a gift; the community, in turn, undertakes the obligation of providing for their sustenance.

Secular priests (or diocesan priests, who are trained in the diocesan seminaries) do not generally make any vow of poverty, and there is no ecclesiastical law which imposes it upon them. Still, there are those who make a private vow of their own, upon the advice of their confessor, before or after their priestly ordination. With this vow they obligate themselves to undertake a life that is similar to that lived by the poor people of their country, and to give away everything superfluous, for works of mercy.

Thus, whether they make a vow or not, all priests are bound, for a great variety of reasons, to labor incessantly towards the ideal of Gospel poverty.

The Church of the Poor

The words of St. Paul: "Those who buy, let them live as though they had no goods, and those who deal with the world as though they had no dealings with it. For the form of this world is passing away" (I Cor. 7, 30-31) are valid for all Christians. The Christian makes an exceptional contribution to social and economic life whenever he succeeds in freeing himself of his self-seeking and his hunger for possessions and becomes capable of making use of the gifts of God's goodness to build up the brotherhood of human society. The priest must be the first to give the example. When he remains too attached to the goods of this world, he is no longer in a position to give a convincing and effective demonstration of his belief in the existence of eternal and imperishable goods.

Moreover, without the spirit of evangelical poverty, how can the priest make people realize that the Church, following the direction of her Divine Founder, is meant to be particularly close to the poor?

The celibacy of the priest is intended to make him free for Christ and for Christ's kingdom. But if the priest shows too great an attachment to the things of earth, he will end up by destroying the value of his celibacy, and depriving it of all its deeper meaning.

The priesthood is the service of the unity of Christ's disciples and it demands that this characteristic trait assume a visible expression in the unity of priests among themselves. It would be contrary to the spirit of this unity for a priest to have a superabundance of temporal goods and not share them with his brothers in the ministry, especially those who work in mission territories.

43

IS THERE ANY MEANING IN THE VOW OF POVERTY?

We must recognize the fact that the spirit of poverty is no longer felt in the Church today as a "vow," but rather as something that is thought about and never practiced. The real poor people are not those who take vows in the religious orders and congregations. The real poor people are in the world. This fact is recognized by the famous French thinker, Georges Bernanos. In his book, Man Alone, *he has to say: "These poor people are there even though we fail at times to recognize them (indeed too often they do not even recognize themselves).*

They make no vow of poverty: it is God himself who makes the vow for them, without their knowing it: He has pierced their hands so that they will remain ever empty...".

Religious orders and congregations as such are moral personalities, like corporations, rich in money and property. For the individual priest or brother or sister there can be no question of personal poverty as such. In theory, yes; in the abstract a solution is easy; but in practice, no! Let's clear up this hypocrisy!

They tell the story of how the Polish Secret Police

(NKWD) one day called upon a young priest, who
enjoyed considerable influence in his work, and proposed
that he operate as a spy for them against the best interests of the Church. If he refused to accept, they threatened to spread the story of how, some years previous,
he had become involved with a young woman who had
given birth to a baby. They also made other threats.

The unfortunate priest begged for a little time to
think it over and promised to give them an answer the
following Sunday after Mass. When Sunday came,
he climbed into the pulpit and, humiliated and ruined,
confessed the sins of his past life to the whole congregation, without omitting a single thing. Then he turned
to leave, explaining that he was no longer worthy to
continue the exercise of his priestly ministry. But while
the Communist police went off furious at the failure of
their clever plans, the parishioners all surrounded their
pastor, of one accord, and testified to their love and
confidence in him. He had confessed his sins publicly
and they were now more than ever aware of how much
goodness was in their priest. He had to face a brave
and very unequal fight against sin and human weakness
in order not to turn into a hypocrite.

Even in the ranks of her priests and her religious the
Church wages a not always victorious campaign for
the spirit of poverty. Still, the sad reality of the fact
that individual religious, individual monasteries, or even
whole religious provinces, sometimes transgress, in a
greater or lesser degree, the poverty they have vowed to
keep, sometimes even brazenly betraying their sacred
trust, cannot induce the Church to renounce the ideal of

voluntary and exemplary poverty. This poverty must always be renewed with humility and courage. The very first step is the humility and courage involved in recognizing and publicly admitting the shortcomings and deviations that have crept into the proper observance of this vow. Then it is time to look for the proper remedies, and the Gospel affords a good outline for this work of reform.

Testimony to Poverty

Love, in some cases, has to cut and burn in order to root out an abscess and effect a cure. It is much better to set the religious free or dismiss him if he does not observe his vows and does not intend to be faithfully converted to the true spirit of their practice, than to force him to remain in a state which can only involve his ingratitude and dishonor. Outside the monastery, where he is forced to earn his bread with his own hands, he might, with the help of God's grace, learn to appreciate the benefit of work and daily concern for his own sustenance. Such an operation is frequently necessary in every religious order. Naturally, even in the monastery there is an obligation and need to support and help those who are weak. But the great mission of religious orders and congregations is precisely the work of giving a convincing testimony of the spirit of poverty and the joy and goodness that always accompany it. That is why it is always necessary to prune away the dry branches and keep the main stock of the community life green and flourishing.

The comforts of our modern society pose many new problems to the Church and to her religious congregations. Religious too have a part to play in the society of our modern times. It is not psychologically possible to claim that they must live like men in the stone age. The congregations whose apostolate is at the service of the modern world can and must make use of the most modern means of our modern times. The decisive element in these cases is the factor of personal disinterestedness, proper behavior, careful attention to keep from turning modern technical progress, etc., into an end in itself, seeking and applying it only in so far as it serves to promote and further the spiritual mission of the congregation.

In the recent Council, we saw many statements about the need for a renewal of the spirit of poverty and simplicity, and many bishops have begun by giving a good example in their personal decisions. The superior general of the religious orders and congregations are seriously taken up with this problem; they are praying and asking for advice in their efforts to find a way to reconcile modern progress in their institutions of apostolic work with the most absolute faithfulness to the real spirit of poverty. For the rest, this is not the first time in history that a great movement of renewal has appealed to the spirit of evangelical poverty. All the great reforms of the Church have always been based upon, and helped to further, a reform in the spirit of poverty. On the other hand, riches, the token and source of earthly power and comfortable living, have never made any contribution to the real good of Church institutions as such.

This frank and outspoken language is nothing new in the Church. This fact can be substantiated by reference to any decent textbook on Church history where these problems have been objectively and courageously treated.

The renewal of the spirit of poverty is, moreover, a problem that interests the whole Church, even if the various vocations require differing degrees of realization of this ideal. We must not be surprised to note that even among the lay people who live in the midst of the world voices have been raised calling for a renewal of this spirit. Still, all this will help the Church only if it is solidly rooted in humility and love, accompanied by good example, and sparked by a personal effort at renewal.

44

SICKNESS AND CHRISTIAN HOPE

I am a very unfortunate mother: I lost two of my children at a very tender age, and my third child, upon whom I had to lavish all my maternal love and care, after an uninterrupted series of sicknesses and complications, at the age of 18, completely lost his reason and had to be sent to an institution. Tell me, now, whether or not

*there is any meaning in the concept of "Chris-
tian hope" for me?*

Some years ago I visited a sick woman who had been
suffering from rheumatism for some 20 years; she had
been confined to her bed without any hope. Her room
was neat and filled with peace. She told me of the
great love and goodness that she always felt. On the
subject of her own sickness she said simply: "Only with
the passage of time can we come to understand what a
blessed thing it is to be able to suffer. How many
people could really help themselves in this way!"

During my visit to the homes in the outlying districts
of a parish in 1948 I arrived at one home in which
there was a family that had, together with several normal,
healthy children, an epileptic child who was completely
retarded. I could see what a burden the child was
upon the entire family. The mother was grateful for
my suggestion that the child be sent to a hospital run
by the religious sisters. But when the conversation
reached the point where we were seriously thinking of
taking the child away, the mother had this to say:
"I cannot let my little one go, for it, of all my children,
has found a special place deep within my husband's
heart and mine."

These are two cases in which Christian hope has
managed to shine triumphantly in the presence of a
hopeless disease. In the first case it is the sick person
herself who has arrived at this full awareness of the
redemptive value of suffering and her own sickness.

In the second, the sickness, even more distressing, has turned into a motive that stimulated and encouraged the full development of Christian hope and love in two parents.

The Essence of Hope

Sickness without hope, from the medical point of view, can cast a very special light on the essence of real Christian hope. Sickness — not in itself, but in virtue of the cross and resurrection of Christ — is a situation which can open the door to real Christian hope.

Bodily and spiritual health, which affords us such a natural joy and well-being, can and should, with the grace of God, turn into a path that leads to Christian hope. For the man who has faith everything can become a pledge and idea of the beatifying love of God; earthly life, the healthy life which faces the future with freshness and joy, can become the harp which sounds the clear and joyfully harmonious strains of our longing for eternal life. Thus the sick person, who has looked earthly death in the eye but then begins to experience the symptoms of recovery, after he has oriented his whole being towards eternal life in the love of God, can see, in this hope he has of an earthly recovery, a more living idea of how much true Christian hope in God has to contribute to maintaining life. Spiritual depression, which many sick people inevitably have to face, is certainly not the best background for the development of a sturdy Christian hope.

Hope in the Cross

To put it briefly: the vitality of Christian hope is partially bound up with those natural goods which seem desirable to us and which make us have greater confidence in our own existence and in the Lord of our destiny. But we must not lose sight of a further truth, equally fundamental: Christian hope shares in the paradox of the cross. This truth has found its classic expression in the Beatitudes of the Sermon on the Mount. To the "poor in spirit" Christ promises the kingdom of God. "Those who mourn" will be called blessed, "because they will be comforted." Certainly, these and the other beatitudes can all be very fruitfully explained on the basis of the principle of self-denial, and the salutary sorrow that proceeds from repentance for our sins, that is to say, in an immediately religious framework. But in the mouth of Christ, who claims to have come to bring the good news to the poor, to raise up those who are burdened and oppressed, it is impossible not to notice a particular love for those who are really poor and, in human terms, have no further hope. The man who is weighed down by original sin is always at a disadvantage; he is always predisposed to look upon these goods of earthly existence as the ultimate realities instead of seeing them as the image and impulse to a more elevated form of Christian hope. Christ, on Good Friday, was forced to shatter all the earthly hopes of his disciples, the choicest spirits among his people, and then, in his Resurrection and Ascension, to open their eyes to the full scope of real Christian hope.

Our Redeemer, in his death on the cross, went so far as to accept the apparent failure of every hope reposing in his work on earth. He even permitted death, which, by reason of original sin, is always bound up with an element of desolation and tragedy, to descend upon him with all its bitterness. He gave his consent with a heart crushed with sorrow. In the extremity of his desolation he confidently entrusted his soul into his Father's hands. His passion and death did not do away with death and suffering on earth. But he did transform death, and, with death, all sickness, expecially the sickness that is humanly without hope, into a road of love and a road of hope.

The Christian meaning of a sickness without hope is not always so clear as in the two cases described above. In fact, these two cases might be said to represent an exception. Still, joined with all the many other cases in which there is at least a small ray of this light of hope shining through, they do reveal the end and meaning of sickness suffered without any human hope.

45

CHRISTIAN HOPE IN THE FACE OF THE ABYSS

I am an invalid with no hope of being cured. Do I have an obligation to submit to painful and useless treatments which involve a good

deal of expense and hardship on my family?
What is the good of it all? I am so tired of
suffering that the only thing I really want is to
see it all over with as soon as possible.

In our modern world of medicine, a refusal of medical
aid in a serious case, for example, leaving it entirely
to God to put an end to our suffering whenever he wants
to, does appear to be the sign of a rather unclear awareness or an unjustifiable lack of confidence in the medical
profession. But are we to condemn also those persons
who, upon learning that they are on the point of death,
predispose themselves to die by refusing all further
medical assistance, even though such a refusal will
cause them to die some time sooner than otherwise?
I do not believe that, from the point of view of Christian
morality, there can be any serious objections to such a
line of conduct since it is not contrary to the behavior
of a person who looks upon life as a gift from God and
thus not foolishly waste it nor senselessly expose it to
danger or unnecessarily shorten it. So far as I know,
Catholic moralists generally admit that there is no
objection against taking drugs to reduce pain and
suffering, even though this sometimes involves a
shortening of life. In a word, we simply are not obliged
to prolong our life, for perhaps a few days, with all
the means at our disposal. In the light of Christian
hope, such a practice, in certain circumstances, seems
to be a sort of madness. Still, it is not morally admissible
to do anything which in some circumstances might,
objectively, take on the character of an attempted flight

from the sufferings of this life, to a personal and onesided decision to put it to an end.   Even negligence or carelessness in this respect might be the expression of one's own deliberate will to put an end to his life.

46

THE DOCTOR'S DUTY

I work in a hospital and frequently I am faced with a sickness that is chronic and for which there is no hope at all. In the course of treating such a desperate case may I limit my attention to the prescription of anti-pain drugs and sedatives, or must I make the same detailed and concentrated effort I would make in the case of a patient who presented good hopes of recovery?

It is impossible to advance solid arguments for the doctor's obligation to prolong life, absolutely, in terms of days and hours and minutes, with all the means at his disposal.   Thus the doctor need not try to keep the patient in a continuous state of unconsciousness, in an effort to prolong his life for a short time.   This might prevent the patient from accepting the prospect of death with dignity.   A Christian doctor, for example, will do everything he can to help a person who has suffered a serious attack and whose chances of surviving are practically null, to recover consciousness at least for a short time and thus prepare for his passage into eternity. This will appear to be more important, in his eyes, than merely making an effort to keep death away for a few more hours or days.

At all events, this does not represent an immediate answer to our problem which presupposes a somewhat different situation. But, on the basis of cases which are nearly similar, it is possible to deduce principles that are of general validity. The doctor has an obligation — to sum up the answer to the question — to use his normal capacity and his normal concern in the case of acute complications which place life in serious danger, even in the case of incurably ill patients, without regard to the fact that the life in question is, or is not, of any immediate usefulness for any purpose whatsoever. It is not the province of the moralist to indicate what this normal measure should be. It is the doctor himself who must decide in terms of the medical science of his day and the normal social demands and needs of the patient.

Still, even in these cases, the doctor is not obliged to make every possible effort to prolong life by a few days, or by a few hours, when death is obviously just around the corner.

Professional Concern

Certainly we are not to blame the doctor, on the other hand, who, in extraordinary cases, such as, for example, the case of a patient who is near and dear to him or a very important person (a mother with several young children, a man with public responsibilities), makes a greater than average effort to effect a cure. Nor would it be any injustice on his part if he were to devote his efforts first and primarily to curing a patient whose illness presented fewer complications and devoted only his remaining hours to the care of a patient who was obviously already well along the road to his death. As a matter of general principle, however, he has an obligation to be concerned equally and regularly, with every life under his care, whether it offers a greater or lesser degree, humanly speaking, of eventual cure and recovery. This is the measure of his respect for human life as such, and for the Lord of all life.

The man who does not accept such principles must attempt to demonstrate the mentality from which the opposite imperatives would derive, and where their logical consequences, in the extreme case, would inevitably lead. In questions like these we must also take into account the depths of the human heart. It is from these depths that, in the last analysis, only Christian hope and the strength of Christian love can offer any salvation.

47

I AM A WIDOW AND CONFUSED

At the age of 28 I lost my husband, and our marriage had never been blessed with children. I do not have the strength to make a new life

> *for myself. I seem to have become a useless*
> *person and existence no longer has any meaning*
> *for me. Everything looks black and it is hard*
> *to make an effort. Can there really be any hope*
> *for a person who suffers pain like this?*

Widowhood, borne with strength of soul, is protected by the shadow of the cross of Christ and the hope of resurrection, the glory of the sacrament of matrimony and the honor of a fidelity that continues beyond the grave. The widow and the widower know from experience what a great blessing conjugal love can be, and they realize it in a new way, by the painful experience of separation, and the death of a loved companion along the path of life.

The suffering of the widow, compared to the bitter sufferings of those who are separated, is a transfigured suffering. The widow has experienced love and fidelity "until death do us part," whereas her unfortunate sister, the divorced woman, has been forced to watch her beloved husband withdraw from her and reject her love.

The woman who has been faithlessly abandoned remains far from the house in which her husband, once entrusted to her alone, now lives with some other woman; all her hopes are buried and betrayed.

The widow, on the other hand, frequently goes to visit the grave of her companion in marriage, whom she continues to love even after death. She knows that he is near to her, in the love of God, and she looks to the cross of Christ which has become the tree of life for all who believe. She looks at the ear of golden grain that

she had carved on the tombstone as a symbol. In her
faith she knows, and her heart repeats it with growing
clarity: "Unless the grain of wheat falls into the earth
and dies, it remains alone; but if it dies, it bears much
fruit" (John 12, 24). She remembers how their mutual
love, in self-renunciation and in seeking each other,
turned into a more and more beautiful and pure and
blessed road to walk together. She comes to understand,
with absolute clarity, that the mortal sickness and the
loss of her husband have effected the final purification
of her love. No matter how painful the physical separation might prove to be, she realizes now, with gratitude,
that, from the very beginning their's was something
more than physical love. Together they have walked
along the path that leads to God. It was on God that
their love was based. In loving each other they raised
each other closer to him, until finally they arrived at a
concrete idea of his love in all its blessedness. Love like
this, in God, cannot ever die.

Love Does Not Die

Sacred Scripture clearly shows the Church's attitude
towards widows. In his first letter to the Corinthians
(7, 39 ff), St. Paul has this to say: "A wife is bound to
her husband as long as he lives. If the husband dies,
she is free to be married to whom she wishes, only in
the Lord. But in my judgment she is happier if she
remains as she is. And I think that I have the Spirit
of God."

The sacrament of matrimony is one form of sharing

in the pact of love existing between Christ and his Church which is the medium of grace; but it is a sharing in a transitory sign. The fact that death breaks this indissoluble bond and allows the surviving party to marry, validly, a second time, also indicates that matrimony is a representation of the new and eternal covenant only in a transitory sign. The Christian will not be preoccupied with his home or with his marriage as if they were the ultimate realities. Out of love for marriage he will not ever sacrifice his own life. On the other hand, marriage, understood in a Christian way, will keep him steadily oriented towards the eternal kingdom of love. In his marriage the eternal is already present, in conjugal love even, which is an image of the love of Christ, a love which, in its more profound content, cannot ever die. The widow, who was granted, in marriage, the living experience and the blessedness of a love that is a sign of heaven, can draw from it the strength it takes to spontaneously renounce the prospect of a new marriage, whenever the circumstances do not demand otherwise. She does this freely, with that freedom that springs from love and blossoms into the blessed liberty of the children of God. Here too we see the full and perfect blessedness of those who have had a share in the sorrow and suffering of Christ, and its capacity to set man free (cf. Matt. 5, 4).

Widowhood freely embraced is an approach to virginity out of love for our Savior: the Council of Trent maintains that this is the more perfect way. It is possible to choose the state of virginity only if a person is interiorly filled with the blessedness of Christ's love. A great Christian teacher, Clement of Alexandria, writes that, by her undivided love for Christ, a widow becomes, in a certain sense, a virgin. This she becomes, however, only "in her own way," that is, in her free and deliberate acceptance of her marriage experience. According to the exhortation of the Apostle, she has received and given, in her marriage, a love which, fundamentally, was a sign of the presence of Christ's life (cf. I Cor. 7, 29); that is why, for the widow, the memory of her marriage and the spiritual heritage that is hers from her marriage is not an obstacle for her joyous love of God, but a way that is well adapted to her. What great blessedness must there not be in the love of God if the love between man and wife, no matter how imperfect, can produce such joy and satisfaction, even beyond the grave.

48

CAN I STILL DO ANY GOOD?

At the age of 42, I became, and have remained, a widow. I have no children. After the despair of those first days, I managed to recover something of my former calm, largely by my faith and prayers. Now that I find myself all alone, I frequently ask: Is there anything I can do, any way to make myself useful at all any more? Can life actually have any more meaning for me?

From the days of the Apostles, the Church has always had a great respect and consideration for widowhood. The Apostle of the Gentiles says expressly: "Honor widows who are real widows." (I Tim. 5, 3). In order to be admitted to the state of widowhood the widow had to pass this simple test which the Church established: "She must be well attested for her good deeds, as one who has brought up children, shown hospitality, washed the feet of the saints, relieved the afflicted, and devoted herself to doing good in every way" (I Tim. 5, 10). The motherly love and goodness of the widow is not to be limited to the inner circle of her family, but it is in the family intimacy that she gives the greatest proofs of what she is: "If a widow has children or grandchildren, let them first learn their religious duty to their own family and make some return to their parents; for this is acceptable in the sight of God" (I Tim. 5, 4). She derives the strength she needs for this activity from her prayer and meditation: "She who is a real widow, and is left all alone, has set her hope on God and continues in supplications and prayers night and day" (I Tim. 3, 5).

Apostolate

Sacred Scripture and the history of the Church present the character of many widows who were really God-fearing women: Judith; the prophetess Anna, who lived in the Temple at the time of Christ; Monica, the mother of St. Augustine; Elizabeth of Thuringia; Brigitta of Sweden. In every age, widows have accomplished great things in the lay apostolate.

Sacred Scripture is not ignorant of the difficulties and dangers facing the widow. Particularly a rather young widow who has not had the good fortune to be married for many years and prove the maturity of the bond of her love, perhaps without children, finding little support and aid among her own relatives, might well run the risk of not understanding the true meaning of her lot in life and not being able to withstand its dangers by herself. She needs the spiritual assistance of her neighbors and the priest. The person who does not feel the call to widowhood might well consider the possibility of a second marriage. But it seems to be more in keeping with the love of the first husband or wife for the widow or widower not to remarry. Still, in concrete cases, such a remarriage might prove to be desirable for many reasons. All this is well expressed in the clear ideas of St. Paul. Today unlike times past, many widows no longer have the support of their former homes and families; thus the eventuality of a second marriage must be considered more frequently.

Widows who, with brave spirit and real courage see to the careful upbringing of their children in a perfect state of widowhood, giving a very precious example of fidelity, patience, and courage, can look forward to more than merely the secret respect that is nurtured in the human heart. They have a right to be honored by their neighbors, and by society. The greater the kindness and admiration shown to widows by those among whom they live, the more easily they will be able to bear their lot in life, to understand and realize the more profound meaning of their destiny: to accept with trust the holy will of God.

49

THE LAY APOSTOLATE

> *I am a layman, 50 years old, with no family obligations. I heard my Pastor explaining the Constitution on the Church as promulgated by the Second Vatican Council, in which there is a good deal of discussion about holiness and the apostolate of the laity. At my age, is there anything I can do?*

There certainly is. Article 41 of the dogmatic constitution, *Lumen Gentium*, is expressly addressed not only to the deacons and clerics but also to "those of the laity, chosen of God, who are called by the bishop in order to devote themselves more completely to apostolic works and who work in the fields of our Lord with much fruit."

Even if the diaconate were to be effectivelly reintroduced as a permanent hierarchical order, there are many other important functions in the Church that can all be filled by non-ordained laymen. Such roles, for instance, as the catechist in mission territories, religion, teacher, director of the Catholic Action, apostle in the charitable activities of the Church, teacher in the Catholic schools,

organist, sacristan, director of Church papers and re-
views, etc. The laymen who fulfill these missions in
conformity with the directives of the bishop who has
called them occupy a position in the Church similar to
that of the clerics, and also enjoy a spirituality that is
very much like theirs. Their road to holiness consists
primarily in this service, in this Church "diaconate"
which exercise in humility and dedication — "diaconate"
(*diaconia*), in the early Church, meant simply service.
If it is men we are discussing, many of them will, no
doubt, in the future, actually be ordained deacons in the
full sense of the word. But it is also, and primarily,
the women of our parishes who, in constantly increasing
numbers, are devoting their time and efforts, without
becoming sisters or religious, to the service of the organized apostolate of the Church.

It is very significant that the constitution felt the
need to call attention, with gratitude, to this service
rendered by the layman, a service which is so precious
and all but impossible to do without.

50

HOLINESS OF THE LAITY

*It is generally said that the saints, in order to
arrive at their perfection, abandoned the world
and consecrated themselves to God in the priestly ministry or in a cloister. Are we lay people,*

*who because of the various obligations and bur-
dens we have freely assumed, and being forced
to live in the world, thus condemned to a life of
inescapable mediocrity?*

The pastoral orientation of the Second Vatican Council
reaches a climax in its teaching on the universal vocation
to holiness. The fifth chapter of the constitution, *Lumen
Gentium,* derives its whole importance and meaning from
the very fact that it is not developing a marginal or
secondary theme. The doctrine that is systematically
developed here is to be found as a guideline and compo-
nent of the entire constitution, and it is echoed in other
constitutions and decrees as well, which illustrate its
principles or develop its conclusions. Under this aspect
we might well say that the Second Vatican Council is
the most "pious" of all the ecumenical councils. Much
more strongly than any of its predecessors, it casts a
very clear light on the sublime dignity and, at the same
time, strictly binding obligation and vocation, of all
Christians, and particularly the laity. All the Council's
work is openly oriented towards the sanctification of the
entire Christian people.

The Paschal mystery — which embraces the passion
and the glorification of Christ as indissolubly united
together — occupies a position of particular preeminence
in the theology of Vatican II, beginning with the decree
on the sacred liturgy. The same direction is taken by
the considerations of the "Church of the poor," which
is witness to God's power as manifest in weakness, in
suffering, and in death. The doctrine on the universal

call to holiness, which occupies such a central position
in the constitution, *Lumen Gentium,* is illuminated by
the whole of the Paschal mystery. There cannot be
any holiness without self-denial, without humility, without effort, and without suffering and pain. That is why
the message of the universal call to holiness — excepting
the call to martyrdom: the martyr sheds his blood to
become like to Christ, in a supreme test, and testimony
of his love — is directed, with special predilection, to
"those who are oppressed by poverty, by weakness, by
sickness and by various tribulations, and to those who
suffer persecution for justice." In this respect, article
41 develops the two great perspectives of Christian
existence: a special participation in the redemptive work
of Christ and the law of life of the beatitudes.

Suffering and Sanctity

The description of the general characteristics of this
call to holiness, as well as the description of the multi-
plicity of these forms of call and vocation, constantly
calls attention to the tension that obtains between "being
in the world" and "not being of this world." Religion
and holiness are life. A person does not become holy
"notwithstanding the fact that he lives in marriage,"
but rather precisely in the fulfillment of his marital
vocation, his role as father or mother. The constitution
does not follow the views of Thomas a Kempis, who
maintains that no one has ever become any better as
the result of sickness. On the contrary, a man can
become holy precisely by his acceptance of the suffering,

poverty, and weakness that come his way, sanctified by
Divine Providence. We can achieve holiness in every
profession and in every honest state of life in the world.
We can live according to the spirit of the Gospel and
its many counsels, even in the midst of the world. Even
though only a minority are called to the religious life
and still have to live in the world, the three counsels
of virginity, spiritual obedience beyond that which is
required of all, and real voluntary poverty — still all are
called to a grateful acceptance of all of God's gifts,
even the goods of earth, with that detachment from
such goods which is a testimony of our faith in the
Paschal mystery and the transitory character of the
"form of this world."

Adequate testimony of the fulness of grace in these
recent times and the holiness of the Church cannot be
the result of the work of any one state or any one form
of vocation no matter how excellent it is; it can result
only from the perfect harmony and concert of all the
saints, the product of every state and every condition
of human life.